TEACHING
EARLY READER
COMICS -AND-GRAPHIC NOVELS

KATIE MONNIN

 Maupin House

Teaching Early Reader Comics and Graphic Novels

By Katie Monnin

Cover illustration: Eric Wight
Cover and book design: Mickey Cuthbertson

Library of Congress Cataloging-in-Publication Data

Monnin, Katie.
 Teaching early reader comics and graphic novels / Katie Monnin.
    p. cm.
 Includes bibliographical references and index.
 ISBN 978-1-936700-23-3 (pbk.)
1. Reading (Early childhood)--United States. 2. Language arts (Early childhood)--United States. 3. Graphic novels. 4. Comic books, strips, etc. I. Title.
 PN6790.U6M66 2011
 372.41'2--dc22

              2011004335

Continue the conversation with Dr. Katie Monnin on her blog, www.teachinggraphicnovels.blogspot.com.

Maupin House publishes professional resources for K-12 educators. Contact us for tailored, in-school training or to schedule an author for a workshop or conference. Visit www.maupinhouse.com for free lesson plan downloads.

Maupin House Publishing, Inc.
2416 NW 71 Place
Gainesville, FL 32653
www.maupinhouse.com
800-524-0634
352-373-5588
352-373-5546 (fax)
info@maupinhouse.com

10 9 8 7 6 5 4 3 2 1

-DEDICATION-

This book is dedicated to teachers.
For every child you inspire, you pay it forward.

-TABLE OF CONTENTS-

-ACKNOWLEDGMENTS-

To my family: You make me a better teacher. Heck, you make me a better person! So, even though "thank you" doesn't seem enough to cover it, "THANK YOU!" (Did all caps help?): Lauren, Henry, Sophie, and Rose Vachon; Mom and Dad (Judy and Ed Monnin); and my brother Andy Monnin and his family.

To Lauren: While at one moment you take my breath away with all of your brilliance and beauty, you inspire me to reach for the stars in the next. You are my very best friend and greatest supporter. You make me believe that the impossible is possible. The unimaginable imaginable. With you, I'm the little engine that always can. You are the most amazingly brilliant and beautiful person to ever walk this earth...Wow, now I hope there aren't any aliens on other planets walking around all beautiful and stuff; if so, I would have to write *universe*. Code: universe.

Samantha (a.k.a.: "Sam-a-lamb") and "Max-handsome" Monnin: Best wiener dogs to ever, ever be wiener dogs! And, yes, wiener dogs can read.

A big "thank you" to the University of North Florida. If anyone is looking for an awesome job at an awesome university in an awesome area of the country that just so happens to be near a few awesome beaches, please consider UNF. UNF is a supportive, collaborative, and beautiful place to spend your time living and working.

I always have a big grin on my face when I talk about Dr. Wanda Hedrick. One of the best conversationalists of all time, Dr. Hedrick is both a mentor and a friend.

I would not be where I am today without Dr. Nancy Padak. Always and forever, thank you for taking me under your wing and teaching me to fly.

Special shout-outs go to the following people for their support: Françoise Mouly, Art Spiegelman, Toon Books, Gina Gagliano, Mark Siegel, First Second Books, Jim Valentino, Dr. James Bucky Carter, Peter Gutierrez, William Kist, Donna Alvermann, and Enrique Puig.

Eric Wight, you rock! Best book cover ever! I am so thankful for your artistic contribution and for your friendship.

And last but certainly not least, thank you to Jane Yolen. Jane, when I was growing up I could only dream about knowing the greatest children's author of all time. Today, dream come true. Thank you for being a caring and inspiring friend. And, especially, thank you for writing the foreword to this book. You inspire me, the literary world, and all the teachers, parents, and students who admire your work each and every day.

-FOREWORD-

JANE YOLEN

Jane Yolen is the author of the graphic novels *Foiled* (First Second), *Curses, Foiled Again* (First Second), and *The Last Dragon* (Dark Horse Comics), as well as *Owl Moon* (Philomel), *How Do Dinosaurs Say Goodnight?* (Scholastic), *The Devil's Arithmetic* (Penguin), and 300 other books.

When I was growing up, those of us who loved comics read intently in one of three kinds—happy comics like *Archie*, superhero comics, and horror comics. We read them squatting down in the drugstore or news-store while Mom or Dad shopped, or sitting in the bathroom with the water running to disguise what we were really doing, or under covers at night with a flashlight.

I read E.C. Comics' *Tales from the Crypt*, all twenty-seven issues. My parents never knew. I borrowed them from a high school (boy)friend, reading them fervently and frantically under the covers, returning them the next day, hidden between the pages of my civics textbook, desperate to get them out of the house before I was discovered. I had my reputation as a smart, literate, good girl to protect, after all.

In a way, that presaged my adult interest in the graphic novel and my reaction to the assumed damage to my literary reputation if it got bruited about that I read comics. I hid my love of Neil Gaiman's *The Books of Magic* and Mike Mignola's *Hellboy*, and Linda Medley's *Castle Waiting* except within the confines of my own house or science-fiction conventions.

But I so wanted to write a graphic novel. And for about fifteen years of trying, the rejections of my ideas for such a project were the same sort of puzzlement I would have gotten if my parents and teachers in the 1950s had known of my interest in comics, especially horror comics. "Why you?" And "We'd rather have a REAL novel from you."

The answer to the "why you" question, which we get from master teacher Katie Monnin's book, is clear. Good girls and boys—and good teachers, too—can love comics and graphic novels; can learn something about literature, art, and reading from the genre; can deepen their understanding of story through graphic novels. Additionally, non-readers can become readers through comics.

And so Dr. Monnin takes us by the hand and leads us pedagogically and practically through the process of demystifying comics and comics reading. She teaches us how to read them without sacrificing a bit of the good girl or good boy label while showing us how to deepen our enjoyment at the same time.

I wish I'd had this book, or a teacher who'd read this book, back when I was in school. But at least I have it now!

-INTRODUCTION-
REDEFINING THE TEACHING OF READING

Sister: Alice! Will you kindly pay attention to your history lesson?

Alice: I'm sorry, but how can one possibly pay attention to a book with no pictures in it?

Sister: My dear child, there are a great many good books in this world without pictures.

Alice: In this world perhaps. But in my world, the books would be nothing but pictures.

- Walt Disney's Alice in Wonderland -

In fourth grade, my teacher's name was Mrs. Savage, an early indication that something wasn't quite right.

Here's the second indication:

"In fourth grade," Mrs. Savage explained, "we DO NOT read kiddie books. No more books with pictures. Time for real reading, ladies and gentlemen!"

In my mind, this translated into two things I could check off my mental list of questions to ask Mrs. Savage:

1. *No need to ask about crayons and markers. If we can't read pictures, we certainly aren't going to be asked to draw or illustrate them.*

2. *No need to ask about recess either. I was pretty certain that while we would want two, like in third grade, Mrs. Savage had probably already decided upon one.*

Mrs. Savage's introduction to fourth grade, while frightening, was also exciting. I had secretly been wishing, as all kids do at some point, that I would be and could be counted as an adult. At the time, I was pretty sure that reading books without pictures and only attending one recess a day meant that I was an adult.

On my revised agenda for that first day of school, I now added: *Inform little brother of new status.*

I got my opportunity at the end of the day on the bus ride home. "Hey, just so you know, I am an adult now, and you are still a baby. I will no longer play with you. Adults don't play with babies."

After I really grew up—which is probably more accurately identified as during my college years rather than in fourth grade—I realized that Mrs. Savage was wrong about reading. And she was certainly wrong about recess.

A READING REVOLUTION: SETTING THE STAGE FOR PRINT-TEXT LITERACIES TO SHARE THE STAGE WITH IMAGE LITERACIES

As an adult reading educator, I have made a career out of being what I call "a scholarly Peter Pan." I still read books with pictures, most of which are graphic novels. And I even travel around to talk to teachers about the contemporary value behind why and how we should intensify our efforts to do so.

So, why do I think it's necessary for teachers to make a shift toward a more visually-based ELA instructional approach?

A shift in ELA pedagogy is necessary because we are living during what many literacy educators see as the greatest communication revolution of all time. In *Literacy in the New Media Age*, Kress (2003) claims that, "The world told is a different world to the world shown" (p. 1). Try to envision a newly built stage with two actors upon it. One character is named Print-text Literacy, and the other is named Image Literacy. On this new-media-age stage, Print-text Literacy and Image Literacy are co-stars. They share the spotlight.

Driven in the last twenty years by a communication revolution second only to the fifteenth-century invention of the printing press, today's ELA teachers are the first generation of educators to redefine the teaching of reading. Today's students live in a new media age, a world where it is critical to be able to read words and images together. Thus, today's reading teacher must teach a shared literacy stage that places emphasis on screen and/or image literacies—computers, televisions, smartphones, email, vmail, videogames, online magazines, the Internet, graphic novels, and comics—alongside print-text literacies. Perhaps Will Eisner (1985), one of the founding fathers of the graphic novel, said it best:

> The format of the comic book presents a montage of both word and image, and the reader is thus required to exercise both visual and verbal interpretive skills. The regimens of art (eg., perspective, symmetry, brush stroke) and the regimens of literature (eg., grammar, plot, syntax) become superimposed upon each other. The reading of the comic book is an act of both aesthetic perception and intellectual pursuit. (*Comics and Sequential Art*, p. 8)

Early reader comics and graphic novels present readers with a rare and modern, literary-level text that uses print-text literacies and image literacies simultaneously. They are invariably independent and dependent upon each other, each one taking center stage at times and then sharing the stage at other times, working in unison to communicate modern, literary stories.

Image literacies such as comics and graphic novels ask us to rethink how we define reading and writing today. The bottom line is that each of these new literacy reading experiences call on us to be competent readers of both words and images; whether looking at a screen or a comic or a graphic novel page, readers must be taught to read images and words together. It's the reality of the world we currently live in.

Eisner (1985) further explains how this new, shared literacy stage has become its own language worthy of classroom attention: "They [comics] become a language—a literary form, if you will. And it is this disciplined application that creates the 'grammar' of Sequential Art" (*Comics and Sequential Art*, p. 8). When we place Eisner's idea that comics and graphic novels are a language worthy of classroom attention within the arguably greatest communication revolution of all time, it becomes abundantly and critically clear that today's educators need to teach this new literary language in their classrooms.

This seismic and exciting shift in ELA pedagogy is revolutionary. Adding image literacies as an equal partner with print-text literacies in ELA classrooms has not only never been attempted, but it has also never been so critically necessary. If we fail to teach print-text literacies alongside image literacies, modern literacy scholars fear that we might commit the greatest disservice in the history of education. Because the literacy world outside of school has so clearly moved on to incorporate print-text literacies alongside image literacies, a failure to adopt a pedagogy of multiliteracies will only create a further gap between what kinds of literacies students interact with at home or at work and those they interact with at school. In our modern era, we cannot afford to gamble on whether or not print-text literacies will ultimately stand the test of time. They won't. Outside of the classroom, the world is already immersed in reading print-text literacies alongside image literacies (Abel & Madden, 2008; Bitz, 2009, 2010; Hadju, 2008; Hull & Schultz, 2002; Kist, 2004, 2010; Masterman, 1985; McCloud, 1993, 2000, 2006; McLuhan, 1964).

Remember: While our current communication revolution is second chronologically, it is first in terms of significance! By shifting our pedagogy away from a solo focus on teaching print-text literacies alone and toward a dual, shared focus on teaching print-text and image literacies together, we are the first generation of teachers to redefine what it means to read. Each and every semester, my pre-service and in-service teachers state that they find this critical time in the history of teaching ELA empowering. In the fall of 2009, an undergraduate student wrote, "I wanted to be a teacher so I could make a difference. Now I get to be part of the most difference ever. It's exciting!" A graduate student sent an email after class was over, which stated: "The class made me look at everything more seriously. I see now how print text and visual text are everywhere, both together and separate. Our lives are full of images and words. It's like I put on a new set of glasses that allowed me to see anew."

Theoretically, the New London Group (1996) sees this opportunity for today's ELA educators as a chance to adopt "a pedagogy of multiliteracies":

> What we term 'mere literacy' remains centered on language only....A pedagogy of multiliteracies by contrast, focuses on modes of representation much broader than language alone....the visual mode of representation may be much more powerful and closely related to language than 'mere literacy' would ever be able to allow. (p. 64)

Due to their equal reliance on print-text and image literacies, early reader comics and graphic novels are two modern literacy formats that easily lend themselves to the adoption of a pedagogy of multiliteracies.

The conventions and styles used in early reader comics and graphic novels (panels, gutters, word balloons, and so on) have actually been evident and well received in children's literature for quite a while. For instance, Maurice Sendak has often been considered an early pioneer of using comic-like panels and gutters in children's literature, especially in *Where the Wild Things Are* (1963) and *In the Night Kitchen* (1970). Even Charles Schulz (creator of *Peanuts*) and Jim Davis (creator of *Garfield*) have enjoyed well-secured places in children's literature when, in reality, their work is much more comic-like than not.

In fact, early reader comics and graphic novels are currently registering on my personal radar as the most exciting area of new literacy growth. For instance, acclaimed graphic novel and comic book visionaries and entrepreneurs Art Spiegelman (Pulitzer Prize-winning graphic novelist of *Maus*) and Françoise Mouly (Art Editor at *The New Yorker*) have started an early reader, classroom-friendly comic book publishing company called Toon Books. The major publishing companies are even starting to support this shift: Scholastic, First Second Books, Image, and legendary "big dogs" DC and Marvel have all started publishing early reader comics and graphic novels. Large bookstore chains such as Barnes & Noble, Borders, and Books-A-Million now have entire sections of their children's literature departments devoted to early reader comic books and graphic novels.

It's an exciting time to teach literacy to early readers indeed! The goal of *Teaching Early Reader Comics and Graphic Novels* is to give teachers the ready-to-use, practitioner-friendly tools they need to embrace multiliteracies and teach the language of comics and graphic novels in their early reader classrooms.

HOW THIS BOOK IS ORGANIZED

This book is organized into two main sections. In the first section, Chapter 1 presents teachers with the theory and terminology for teaching early reader comics and graphic novels in their classrooms. Chapters 2 through 4 comprise the second section and offer a variety of classroom-friendly ideas for teaching early reader comics and graphic novels to emerging and striving readers (Chapter 2), to advanced readers (Chapter 3), and, finally, for multicultural responsibility (Chapter 4). Each chapter features:

- Grade-level- and age-appropriate comic and graphic novel grab bags: Suggested comics and graphic novels for kindergarten through sixth grade;

- Alignment to the IRA (International Reading Association) and NCTE (National Council of Teachers of English) standards;

- Reading- and writing-focused lesson plans for teaching early reader comics and/or graphic novels;

- A teacher resources section that focuses on a specific early reader comic or graphic novel, its author(s) and illustrator(s), and teaching strategies;

- Classroom-friendly, ready-to-copy blank lesson plans, which can also be downloaded at http://teachinggraphicnovels.blogspot.com.

With hats off and a humble bow to the comic and graphic novel scholars and teachers who have come before me, I offer *Teaching Early Reader Comics and Graphic Novels*.

-CHAPTER 1-
TEACHING EARLY READER COMIC AND GRAPHIC NOVEL TERMINOLOGY

"Hey, do you remember where we put all our comic books?"
- Katie Monnin to her little brother, circa 2001 -

BASIC TERMINOLOGY FOR TEACHING EARLY READER COMICS AND GRAPHIC NOVELS

One of my most vibrant memories of writing *Teaching Graphic Novels* (2010) is deciding upon the necessary terminology teachers would need to know in order to both read and teach graphic novels in their secondary ELA classrooms. "In what ways," I asked myself, "have I taught the graphic novel alongside the mandated secondary English language arts curriculum?"

The answer: To teach comics and graphic novels, I needed to merge my understanding of teaching print-text literacies in ELA with a new understanding of (and appreciation for!) teaching image literacies in ELA. With this merger came an entire chapter devoted to the terminology teachers would need to know in order to both read and teach graphic novels. In a similar vein, but with early reader teachers in mind, I will also outline the significant terminology teachers will need to know in order to both read and teach early reader comics and graphic novels. Depending on the ability level of your students, you will want to choose between a simple, basic set of terms for reading comics and graphic novels (perhaps kindergarten through third grade) or a more complex, layered set of terms for reading comics and graphic novels (perhaps grades four through six). I will detail both choices.

To teach early readers some basic terms for reading comics and graphic novels, you will want to highlight the following: panel, gutter, and balloon (see Figure 1.1). See Appendix A and Appendix B for a copy-friendly listing of the basic and advanced definitions and accompanying examples of panels, gutters, and balloons to use with students.

Panel: The boundary and the contents within it that tell a piece of the story.

Here's an example of a panel from *Benny and Penny in Just Pretend* (Toon Books, 2008) by Geoffrey Hayes.

In this panel example, Penny is looking for her brother Benny. You can see a visual boundary placed around the piece of the story being told. This boundary constitutes the panel.

Gutter: The space between the panels where readers connect two or more ideas into one idea.

Let's look at some gutter examples from *Luke on the Loose* (Toon Books, 2009) by Harry Bliss.

In the first panel, on the top left, readers see Luke's father reporting his lost son to a policeman. Traveling through the gutter and into the second panel, readers next see Luke's father showing the policeman his son's photo. These two panels are linked from one moment to the next moment, from Luke's father reporting his lost son to Luke's father showing the policeman a photo of his son.

Balloons: Usually found inside of a panel, balloons typically create visual boundaries that progress the story in terms of dialogue, thought, and/or sound.

Here's an example of a grouping of balloons from *Adventures in Cartooning* (First Second, 2009) by James Sturm, Andrew Arnold, and Alexis Frederick-Frost.

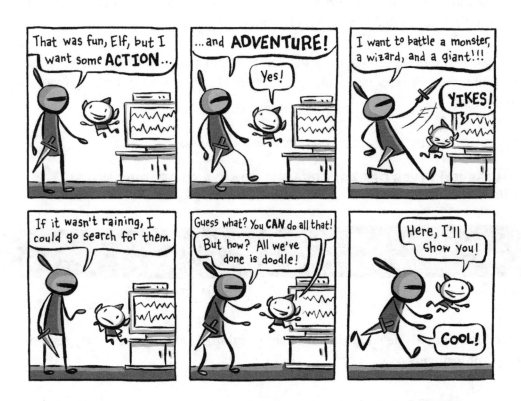

In this example, the knight has specific ideas, each of which manifests itself in a balloon. The magic elf is also shown with some balloons.

ADVANCED, LAYERED TERMINOLOGY FOR TEACHING EARLY READER COMICS AND GRAPHIC NOVELS

Panel: The visual or implied boundary and the contents within it that tell a piece of the story.

Using the *Benny and Penny* panel example from the previous section, let's take a more in-depth look at how panels relate to what we have traditionally taught in ELA.

When we bring our understanding of teaching ELA together with a new understanding of and appreciation for early reader comic and graphic novel panels, we can link the teaching of panels with the teaching of the elements of a story.

For advanced early readers, there are seven types of story panels (Figure 1.2).

FIGURE 1.2: **THE SEVEN TYPES OF EARLY READER COMIC AND GRAPHIC NOVEL STORY PANELS**

SEVEN TYPES OF STORY PANELS FOUND IN EARLY READER COMICS AND GRAPHIC NOVELS

Examples taken from *Benny and Penny in Just Pretend* (Toon Books, 2008) by Geoffrey Hayes.

1. **Plot panels: These panels develop the main set of events that unfold in early reader comics or graphic novels.**

On this first page, Penny is shown looking for her brother, Benny. This initial search is the first in a sequence of events that progresses the storyline.

2. Character panels: These panels focus on and develop individual or multiple characters.

While Benny wants Penny to take her nap and leave him alone, Penny would like to stay and play. A healthy dose of sibling rivalry is clearly at play between these two characters.

3. Setting panels: These panels develop setting, the place(s) where the graphic novel takes place.

While Benny is hidden in his pirate cave, Penny is looking for him from above, near the large tree. The reader can also see that, due to a spider, Benny is about to move to another, new setting in upcoming panels.

4. Conflict panels: These panels develop the source of conflict in the graphic novel, the tension that motivates the story.

In this conflict-focused panel, Benny is revealing the primary tension that runs throughout this story—that he would like to play pirate alone, without his sister.

5. Rising action panels: These panels develop the set of events that stem from the conflict, give rise to that conflict, and lead to the climax in the graphic novel.

Developing the action in the story, Benny tells Penny that he wants to play hide-and-seek. However, in reality, Benny just wants to get away from Penny so he again can play pirate by himself.

6. Climax panels: These panels develop the point of greatest intensity in the story.

After feeling poorly about leaving Penny in the box, Benny goes in search of his sister, and they agree to play "hide-and-seek" together. In these climactic panels, Penny actually proves herself to be much braver than Benny had assumed.

7. Resolution panels: These panels develop the final outcome that solves the primary conflict(s) in the graphic novel.

In the resolution panels, Benny apologizes to Penny.

Gutter: The space between the panels; here, in the limbo of the gutter, human imagination takes over and discovers a logical bridge from one panel to the next panel.

For readers in kindergarten through third grade, I recommend that you refer to the term "gutter" alone.

For readers in grades four through six, however, I recommend that you not only refer to the term "gutter," but also to the five most common types of gutters.

FIGURE 1.3: **FIVE COMMON TYPES OF GUTTERS**

FIVE COMMON TYPES OF GUTTERS

Moment-to-moment gutter: From one panel to the next, readers witness little closure and instead simply see something from one instance to another.

In this example, the reader sees Luke's dad from one moment to the next, first with his cell phone ringing, then as he answers the phone, and, finally, as he begins to talk on the phone.

Examples taken from *Luke on the Loose* (Toon Books, 2009) by Harry Bliss.

Action-to-action gutter: Between these panels, readers see a single subject going through specific transitions.

These gutter sequences show the action generated from Luke chasing the dog.

Subject-to-subject gutter: While sticking with a single idea, these panels move the reader from one subject to the next, often progressing the storyline. McCloud reminds us to "note the degree of reader involvement necessary to render these transitions meaningful" (71).

In the first panel, Luke is the subject. In the second panel, however, Luke's father is the subject.

Scene-to-scene gutter: In reading these panels, readers often need to exercise deductive reasoning, for these panels move the reader across "significant distances of time and space" (McCloud, p. 71, 1993).

The reader moves from the first panel, focusing on Luke's mom as the subject, to the second panel, focusing on Luke as the subject.

Aspect-to-aspect gutter: Because these gutters ask readers to think about the feelings or emotions being conveyed from one panel to the next, they are comparable to tone or mood.

In the top three panels that overlay the larger panel page, the reader gets a sense of the flat or boring parent-to-parent conversational tone. In the page-sized panel, however, the reader gets quite a different tone or mood from Luke—one of excitement.

Note: Students should be encouraged to notice that some gutters can have multiple labels.

Balloons: Usually found inside of a panel, balloons are typically used to create visual boundaries that progress the story in terms of dialogue, thought, and/or sound.

Just like with gutters, for readers in kindergarten through third grade, I recommend that you refer to the term "balloon" alone.

For readers in grades four through six, however, I recommend that you not only refer to the term "balloon," but also to the five most common types of balloons (see Figure 1.4).

FIGURE 1.4: **FIVE COMMON TYPES OF EARLY READER COMIC AND GRAPHIC NOVEL BALLOONS**

FIVE COMMON TYPES OF EARLY READER COMIC AND GRAPHIC NOVEL BALLOONS

Story balloons: Balloons that focus on progressing the storyline/plot.

In these balloons, the reader learns that Otto's favorite color is orange and that, according to Otto, the world would be boring without it.

Example taken from *Otto's Orange Day* (Toon Books, 2009) by Frank Cammuso and Jay Lynch.

Thought balloons: Balloons that focus on a character's thoughts/ideas.

In this thought balloon, which contains a light bulb image, the reader can see that the young knight has thought of an idea.

Example taken from *Adventures in Cartooning* (First Second, 2009) by James Sturm, Andrew Arnold, and Alexis Frederick-Frost.

Dialogue balloons: Balloons that focus on conversation between characters or one character speaking aloud to him/herself.

In these dialogue balloon examples, the reader can see Kaput and Zösky talking about the planet Earth and their desire to get rid of it and eat all the chocolate desserts.

Example taken from *Kaput and Zösky* (First Second, 2008) by Lewis Trondheim and Eric Cartier.

Sound effect balloons: Balloons that use words or images to convey a sense of sound.

Each of these two panels contains a sound effect balloon, with a third sound effect balloon sitting right in between them. They allow the reader to not only hear the characters' grunts as they pull on a costume, but also the rip of the costume as it tears into two pieces.

Example taken from *Mo and Jo: Fighting Together Forever* (Toon Books, 2008) by Dean Haspiel and Jay Lynch.

Balloon-less balloons: Spaces within a panel that have implied boundaries; the balloon-less balloon may also serve any of the aforementioned functions (e.g., a balloon-less story balloon, a balloon-less thought balloon, a balloon-less dialogue balloon).

This balloon-less balloon simply exists within the panel and, due to its focus on purely progressing the storyline, is a story balloon.

Example taken from *Adventures in Cartooning* (First Second, 2009) by James Sturm, Andrew Arnold, and Alexis Frederick-Frost.

Note: Students should be encouraged to notice that some balloons can have multiple labels.

-CHAPTER 2-

TEACHING EARLY READER COMICS AND GRAPHIC NOVELS TO EMERGING AND STRIVING READERS

> **"'Second to the right, and straight on till morning.'
> That, Peter had told Wendy, was the way to the Neverland..."**
> *- Peter Pan -*

At the beginning of a course entitled "Foundations of Literacy," the first in a series of three literacy courses taken by our pre-service elementary education majors at the University of North Florida, students are asked to recall stories about how they learned to read. Anecdotes about loved ones who created character voices and even built stages for enacting stories typically fill the air. These stories always remind me of Peter Pan telling Wendy how to find Neverland.

Experiment, play, and believe in reading, children, and it will take you places.

For most pre-service teachers, learning to read was a pleasant, often enjoyable time when they felt encouraged to dream beyond themselves and the world they knew. But when asked "Did you like learning to read in school?" the sharing session often turns sour.

Here's a sampling of what was shared this past semester:

When little, I liked to read. At school it got horrible.

Reading was fun until Ms. _____'s class in third grade.

Mrs. _____ was the only teacher who knew what we liked to read. She even let us color and draw. She did say she could not let us read what we liked, not even draw what we liked though, because "they" wouldn't let her and it wasn't "really reading."

One of my most ardent hopes for the students in the Foundations of Literacy course is that they are the last generation of students to remember such a dichotomous relationship between what Langer's (1986) research describes as reading for *self* and reading for *school*.

You will notice that this chapter is divided into sections for kindergarten and first grade, second and third grade, and striving—or struggling—readers. These divisions are suggested guidelines only. You know your particular students best and can decide, for example, whether your younger readers can tackle a lesson or book suggested for higher grades.

TEACHING EARLY READER COMICS AND GRAPHIC NOVELS IN KINDERGARTEN AND FIRST GRADE

Kindergarten and first-grade teachers now have the opportunity to be the first generation of teachers to create the building blocks that link reading for school and reading for self.

With comics and graphic novels receiving new, positive attention from a variety of angles, the question for teachers then becomes: When teaching modern students to read, how can we begin to build upon this growing interest in early reader comic books and graphic novels?

Focused on kindergarten and first-grade readers, here's our first "grab bag" (Figure 2.1).

FIGURE 2.1: COMIC BOOK AND GRAPHIC NOVEL GRADE-LEVEL GRAB BAG: KINDERGARTEN AND FIRST GRADE

Baby Mouse: Beach Babe by Jennifer L. Holm and Matthew Holm (Random House, 2006)*

Banana Tail's: Colorful Adventures by Mark McKenna (Image Comics, 2010)

Benny and Penny in Just Pretend by Geoffrey Hayes (Toon Books, 2008)*

Benny and Penny in the Big No-No! by Geoffrey Hayes (Toon Books, 2009)*

Benny and Penny in the Toy Breaker by Geoffrey Hayes (Toon Books, 2010)*

Chicken and Cat by Sara Varon (Scholastic Press, 2006)

Jack and the Box by Art Spiegelman (Toon Books, 2008)

Little Mouse Gets Ready by Jeff Smith (Toon Books, 2009)

Luke on the Loose by Harry Bliss (Toon Books, 2009)

Mo and Jo: Fighting Together Forever by Dean Haspiel and Jay Lynch (Toon Books, 2008)*

My Grandparents Are Secret Agents by Scott Christian Sava (Idea & Design Works, 2009)

Night of the Bedbugs by Paul Fricke (Image Comics, 2010)

Oops by Arthur Geisert (Houghton Mifflin, 2006)

Silly Lilly and the Four Seasons by Agnès Rosenstiehl (Toon Books, 2008)

Squish #1: Super Amoeba by Jennifer Holm and Matthew Holm (Random House, 2011)*

Stinky by Eleanor Davis (Toon Books, 2008)

The Lonely Little Monster by Andi Green (Monsters in My Head, 2007)*

The Three Pigs by David Wiesner (Clarion Books, 2001)

Tuesday by David Wiesner (Sandpiper, 1991)**

* Part of a series

** Caldecott winner

Once you have chosen an early reader comic or graphic novel for your students, you can next identify the major IRA/NCTE standards that align to teaching that literature in kindergarten and first grade. The three most applicable IRA/NCTE standards are:

Standard 1

"Students read a wide range of print and non-print texts to build an understanding of texts, of themselves, and of the cultures of the United States and the world."

Standard 2

"Students read a wide range of literature from many periods in many genres to build an understanding of the many dimensions (e.g., philosophical, ethical, aesthetic) of human experience."

Standard 3

"Students apply a wide range of strategies to comprehend, interpret, evaluate, and appreciate texts. They draw on their prior experience, their interactions with other readers and writers, their knowledge of word meaning and of other texts, their word identification strategies, and their understanding of textual features."

With these standards noted, you can next develop your lesson plans. And even though it is exciting to dive right in, I recommend that you first acquaint students with the terminology for reading comics and graphic novels. Appendix A presents a copy-friendly resource for doing so. Dependent upon the ability level of your readers, you may want to choose between:

1. A focus on either the basic definition of panel, gutter, and balloon, or
2. A focus on the basic and layered definitions of panel (and the various types of panels), gutter (and the various types of gutters), and balloon (and the various types of balloons).

Once this basic or layered terminology is distributed to students and discussed, you can really start to develop more fruitful comic book and graphic novel lesson plans. Armed with their new terminology, kindergarten and first-grade readers are now ready to pair this fresh knowledge with a love for reading in general.

I recommend using a guided-reading (Fountas and Pinnell, 1996) lesson plan structure. Figures 2.2 (before-reading strategies), 2.3 (during-reading strategies), and 2.4 (after-reading strategies) present a variety of reading strategies you may choose from in order to build a guided-reading lesson plan appropriate for your students.

FIGURE 2.2: **THREE BEFORE-READING STRATEGIES FOR KINDERGARTEN AND FIRST-GRADE READERS OF EARLY READER COMICS AND GRAPHIC NOVELS**

KINDERGARTEN AND FIRST-GRADE BEFORE-READING STRATEGIES	EXPLANATION
"What Do You Think?"	For this reading strategy, ask students what they think good readers do when they read. Record or take notes of student responses on the board. **IRA/NCTE standard alignment: Standards 1, 2, and 3.**
Cover Talk	Ask students to discuss what they see on the cover of the book and what this cover might tell them about the story. **IRA/NCTE standard alignment: Standards 1, 2, and 3.**
Point and Share	Point out important concepts of print, including, but not limited to: appropriate ways to hold a book; book title; author's name; book spine; story beginning, middle, and end. As you point to each print concept, modeling for your students, ask them to also hold up their books and point to the same place you are pointing. When everyone is pointing to the same place, share the print concept term and ask students to repeat that term on their own. You will also want to point out and teach concepts of print particular to comics and graphic novels: panels, gutters, and balloons. **IRA/NCTE standard alignment: Standards 1, 2, and 3.**

Once they have completed a before-reading strategy or two, students are next ready to work through during-reading strategies. The following three during-reading strategies fit well alongside any of the before-reading strategies previously suggested in Figure 2.2.

FIGURE 2.3: **THREE DURING-READING STRATEGIES FOR KINDERGARTEN AND FIRST-GRADE READERS OF EARLY READER COMICS AND GRAPHIC NOVELS**

KINDERGARTEN AND FIRST-GRADE DURING-READING STRATEGIES	EXPLANATION
Echo Reading	Read slowly and ask students to repeat or echo what you have read. In terms of early reader comics and graphic novels, you will want to not only read the words, but also read the panels, gutters, and balloons. You may find yourself saying things like: "The first panel shows a character sitting in a chair"; "The gutter between the first and second panel pans out and shows the reader that the character is sitting in a chair in her classroom"; or "The balloon in the second panel says that the character is sighing." **IRA/NCTE standard alignment: Standards 1, 2, and 3.**
Retelling	Divide the story into three sections: beginning, middle, and end. After reading each section, ask students to "retell" that section of the story. **IRA/NCTE standard alignment: Standards 1, 2, and 3.**
TPS: Think, Pair, Share, (with a Prediction Focus)	Stop at different moments in the story and ask students to predict what they think will happen next: • First, ask students to **THINK** to themselves, writing down their predictions about what might happen next. Specifically, given the panels, gutters, and balloons they have read so far, students should think about what might happen in the upcoming panels, gutters, and balloons. • Next, ask students to **PAIR** up with a peer and discuss their predictions. • Then, ask students to **SHARE** their various predictions with the whole class, mentioning specific panels, gutters, and balloons that aided in their predictions. Repeat the **TPS** process as many times as needed. **IRA/NCTE standard alignment: Standards 1, 2, and 3.**

After working through a before-reading strategy and a during-reading strategy, students are ready for an after-reading strategy (Figure 2.4).

FIGURE 2.4: **THREE AFTER-READING STRATEGIES FOR KINDERGARTEN AND FIRST-GRADE READERS OF EARLY READER COMICS AND GRAPHIC NOVELS**

AFTER-READING STRATEGIES FOR KINDERGARTEN AND FIRST-GRADE READERS	EXPLANATION
Art Talks	Using panels, gutters, and balloons, students should highlight a significant moment or event from the story. When finished, students can take turns explaining the significance behind their artwork decisions, specifically noting their panel, gutter, and balloon choices. **IRA/NCTE standard alignment: Standards 1, 2, and 3.**
Felt Story Board	After students are done reading, place a large felt board up front in the center of the classroom. Next, introduce students to pre-made felt characters, panels, balloons, settings, and plot points from the story. Once students understand what each pre-made felt character or event stands for, ask them to help you put the characters and/or events in the order in which they appeared in the story. **IRA/NCTE standard alignment: Standards 1, 2, and 3.**
Reaction Guide	After reading, ask students to react to the story by writing/drawing about the main idea. If they choose to draw, students need to use panels, gutters, and balloons. When finished, have students discuss their individual drawings or reactions. **IRA/NCTE standard alignment: Standards 1, 2, and 3.**

TEACHER RESOURCES FOR KINDERGARTEN AND FIRST GRADE

This chapter's teacher resources for kindergarten and first grade include:

1. A comic book exposé of Geoffrey Hayes' *Benny and Penny in Just Pretend* (Figure 2.5),
2. An example guided-reading lesson plan that focuses on *Benny and Penny in Just Pretend* (Figure 2.6), and
3. A blank guided-reading lesson plan for your classroom use (Figure 2.7).

FIGURE 2.5: **EARLY READER COMIC EXPOSÉ OF *BENNY AND PENNY IN JUST PRETEND***

Benny and Penny in Just Pretend by Geoffrey Hayes (Toon Books, 2008)

Summary

Busy pretending to be a pirate and commanding the seas, Benny is in no mood to play with his cry-baby little sister, Penny. But when Penny goes missing, Benny finds himself just a little concerned. But just a little. Will Benny the Pirate be able to find Penny? Is Penny really a cry-baby?

Interesting information

Goeffrey Hayes has been creating children's books since 1976. Growing up in San Francisco, Hayes and his brother both loved (and still do!) to create comics. Some other popular titles by Hayes include *Bear by Himself*, the *Otto and Uncle Tooth Mystery Readers* series, and the *Patrick Bear* series. Hayes illustrated Margaret Wise Brown's *When the Wind Blew*.

The brilliant storytelling of Geoffrey Hayes has found its way into more than forty publications for children. *Benny and Penny in Just Pretend* was the first Toon Book released. In addition to many outstanding reviews, *Benny and Penny in Just Pretend* has won a number of awards:

- *Booklist* Top 10 Graphic Novels for Youth
- Iowa Goldfinch Award
- Maryland Blue Crab Young Readers Honor Book
- Bank Street College of Education's Best Children's Book of the Year
- Kirkus Reviews Best of 2009 Continuing Series

Due to *Benny and Penny's* success, Hayes wrote two follow-up stories: *Benny and Penny in the Big No-No!* and *Benny and Penny in the Toy Breaker*. Here are some thoughts from Hayes on the value of comics:

> "What I love about comics are their immediacy. Having the words and pictures integrated gives each more life. I also love telling a story sequentially and designing the page layouts to reflect what is being communicated, so that action, word bubbles, color, and composition contribute to getting the meaning across. It's my hope that Benny and Penny will inspire kids to create their own picture-stories and impress upon them that visual storytelling can be as subtle and as literary and enriching as traditional storytelling."

Since Geoffrey Hayes' *Benny and Penny in Just Pretend* has won numerous awards and always seems to be a favorite among early readers, I would like to highlight this text in an example guided-reading lesson plan for your classroom use (Figure 2.6).

FIGURE 2.6: **EXAMPLE GUIDED-READING LESSON PLAN USING *BENNY AND PENNY IN JUST PRETEND***

EXAMPLE GUIDED-READING LESSON PLAN FOR KINDERGARTEN AND FIRST-GRADE READERS	EXPLANATION
Before Reading	**Cover Talk** Ask students to discuss what they see on the cover of the book and what this cover might tell them about the story. In order for students to express their own ideas on what might happen in *Benny and Penny in Just Pretend*, provide some options from Appendix C, "iCreate Comics and Graphic Novels," which will allow students to look at the cover and use words and images to express their predictions about the story. Here are some questions to have students consider and then, in response, write and draw about: • Which character do you think is Benny? • What character do you think is Penny? • What do you think might happen in this story about Benny and Penny? • Why do you think the title includes the word *pretend*? **IRA/NCTE standard alignment: Standards 1, 2, and 3.**

During Reading	**Retelling** Divide the story into three sections: beginning, middle, and end. After reading the beginning of *Benny and Penny in Just Pretend*, present students with more options from "iCreate Comics and Graphic Novels" (Appendix C) and ask them to retell what happened by drawing and writing the story so far (up to each prediction point). Repeat the same process when students reach the middle and the end of the story. Students can then share their retellings with each other, explaining why they made their decisions. **IRA/NCTE standard alignment: Standards 1, 2, and 3.**
After Reading	**Reaction Guide** After reading, ask students to react to the story by writing/drawing the main thematic idea. Again, students can use Appendix C handouts to demonstrate their understanding of the overall story. Have students consider the following questions as they draw and write about the main idea: • What happened to Benny in this story? • What happened to Penny in this story? • What happens to Benny and Penny at the end of the story? When completed, have students discuss their individual reactions as a class. **IRA/NCTE standard alignment: Standards 1, 2, and 3.**

Along with using this example guided-reading lesson plan in the classroom, I also encourage you to create your own lesson ideas. For that reason, a blank guided-reading lesson plan for your classroom use can be found in Figure 2.7. Additionally, share your creative and thought-provoking ideas online at http://teachinggraphicnovels.blogspot.com.

GUIDED-READING LESSON PLAN FOR KINDERGARTEN AND FIRST-GRADE READERS	EXPLANATION
Before Reading	IRA/NCTE standard alignment: Standards 1, 2, and 3
During Reading	IRA/NCTE standard alignment: Standards 1, 2, and 3
After Reading	IRA/NCTE standard alignment: Standards 1, 2, and 3

TEACHING EARLY READER COMICS AND GRAPHIC NOVELS IN SECOND AND THIRD GRADE

One of the most frequent questions I am asked about teaching early reader comics and graphic novels comes from second- and third-grade teachers. They typically want to know how this genre can "pair up" with or help "transition" students to "real reading." Brilliantly intuitive, this question pinpoints a critical and traditional transition point in teaching early readers.

Although second- and third-grade teachers have traditionally been called upon to move students away from picture books and toward traditional, print-text literature, our current communication revolution calls on these teachers to rethink this movement. As discussed in the Introduction, today's reading teachers are the first generation of educators to redefine the teaching of reading on a global, multi-modal scale. As we learned earlier, it is no longer practical—at any grade level—to move students away from picture books and toward print-text literacies alone (Buckingham, 2003; Kist, 2004, 2009; Kress, 2003; The New London Group, 1996).

Second and third grade is now a time to further embrace and empower students to be readers of both print-text literacies and image literacies. The bottom line is, when it comes to teaching reading, second- and third-grade teachers have a new, more contemporary objective during this new media age: To select and embrace texts that rely on both image and print-text literacies.

Thus, in this chapter, I will continue to concentrate on how to shift pedagogy away from a focus on print-text literacies alone and, instead, toward a focus on print-text literacies and image literacies together.

Let's look at another comic book and graphic novel grade-level grab bag.

Baby Mouse: Beach Babe by Jennifer L. Holm and Matthew Holm (Random House, 2006)*

Banana Tail's: Colorful Adventures by Mark McKenna (Image Comics, 2010)

Benny and Penny in Just Pretend by Geoffrey Hayes (Toon Books, 2008)*

Benny and Penny in the Big No-No! by Geoffrey Hayes (Toon Books, 2009)*

Benny and Penny in the Toy Breaker by Geoffrey Hayes (Toon Books, 2010)*

Chicken and Cat by Sara Varon (Scholastic Press, 2006)

G-Man by Chris Giarrusso (Image Comics, 2010)*

Jack and the Box by Art Spiegelman (Toon Books, 2008)

Little Mouse Gets Ready by Jeff Smith (Toon Books, 2009)

Luke on the Loose by Harry Bliss (Toon Books, 2009)

Mo and Jo: Fighting Together Forever by Dean Haspiel and Jay Lynch (Toon Books, 2008)*

My Grandparents Are Secret Agents by Scott Christian Sava (Idea & Design Works, 2009)

Night of the Bedbugs by Paul Fricke (Image Comics, 2010)

Oops by Arthur Geisert (Houghton Mifflin, 2006)

Silly Lilly and the Four Seasons by Agnès Rosenstiehl (Toon Books, 2008)

Squish #1: Super Amoeba by Jennifer Holm and Matthew Holm (Random House, 2011)*

Stinky by Eleanor Davis (Toon Books, 2008)

The Lonely Little Monster by Andi Green (Monsters in My Head, 2007)*

The Smurf King by Peyo (Papercutz, 2010)*

The Three Pigs by David Wiesner (Clarion Books, 2001)

Tuesday by David Wiesner (Sandpiper, 1991)**

* Part of a series
** Caldecott winner

With an early reader comic book or graphic novel selected, you will next want to introduce students to one of the terminology choices found in Appendix A or Appendix B (basic or advanced). When students understand this terminology, you can then think about alignment. The following four IRA/NCTE standards are most applicable to teaching early reader comics and graphic novels in second and third grade.

Standard 1

"Students read a wide range of print and non-print texts to build an understanding of texts, of themselves, and of the cultures of the United States and the world."

Standard 2

"Students read a wide range of literature from many periods in many genres to build an understanding of the many dimensions (e.g., philosophical, ethical, aesthetic) of human experience."

Standard 3

"Students apply a wide range of strategies to comprehend, interpret, evaluate, and appreciate texts. They draw on their prior experience, their interactions with other readers and writers, their knowledge of word meaning and of other texts, their word identification strategies, and their understanding of textual features."

Standard 5

"Students employ a wide range of strategies as they write and use different writing process elements appropriately to communicate with different audiences for a variety of purposes."

Just like with the kindergarten and first-grade section, this section will build upon the most applicable IRA/NCTE standards for teaching early reader comics and graphic novels by recommending various options for guided-reading lesson plans.

SECOND- AND THIRD-GRADE BEFORE-READING STRATEGIES	EXPLANATION
Intermediate Literacy Ladder	Since second- and third-grade teachers have traditionally been called upon to move students away from books with pictures and toward print-text literacy alone, the literacy ladder focuses on building upon students' experiences with picture books. Ultimately, the goal of the literacy ladder is to help students understand how print-text literacies and image literacies now work together to tell all levels of story, both for children and adults. To start the literacy ladder strategy, draw a simple, three-step ladder on the board. On the first step of the ladder, write "Picture Books," and draw a simple image of a picture book. On the second step, write "Comics and/or Graphic Novels," and draw a simple image of both. On the third step, write "Cartoons, Animation, Movies, or Anime," and, once again, draw a simple image of each. Discuss each step of the ladder with students, offering examples of each as you do so. As a class, discuss the following: • Why is the picture book on the bottom step? • Have you ever seen a panel, gutter, or balloon in a picture book? • Why are comics and/or graphic novels on the next step? • Have you ever seen a panel, gutter, or balloon in a comic or graphic novel? • Why are cartoons, animation, movies, or anime on the top step? • Have you ever seen a panel, gutter, or balloon in a cartoon, in a movie, or in anime? Keep a list of student responses on the board. **IRA/NCTE standard alignment: Standards 1, 2, and 3**

Animated Schema	Introduce the main topic behind the early reader comic or graphic novel by first putting the main idea (word/phrase) on the board. Then ask students to read a section of the comic or graphic novel that you have pre-selected. Discuss students' initial thoughts on that topic, and ask them to identify and discuss some of the panels, gutters, and balloons they found. Next, show a short, animated clip/episode that also deals with that topic. Finally, discuss, compare, and contrast what students learned about that topic from the animated episode/clip vs. the comic or graphic novel. Ask students to note any panels, gutters, or balloons they saw in either example. **IRA/NCTE standard alignment: Standards 1, 2, and 3**
Guest Speaker	Find a community stakeholder who has expert knowledge on the topic from the early reader comic or graphic novel. Ask that person to speak to the class and introduce the topic, noting his or her own experiences with comics and graphic novels if possible. Note: Please allow time for questions and answers. Because a question-and-answer period allows students to personally interact with the speaker/topic, they will be more likely to feel engaged by the topic and connected to it. This question and answer period will also help foster future critical thinking (prediction, inference, and sequencing) about reading panels, gutters, and balloons when students start to read the text. **IRA/NCTE standard alignment: Standards 1, 2, and 3**

Once the early reader comic book or graphic novel has been introduced to students with a before-reading strategy, it is now time to think about a during-reading strategy. Because second- and third-grade teachers have traditionally been asked to move students toward print-text literacy alone, I will explain how some of the most common, familiar, during-reading strategies for print text can now be applied to reading both print text and image text together (see Figure 2.10).

SECOND- AND THIRD-GRADE DURING-READING STRATEGIES	EXPLANATION
Popcorn Reading	Popcorn reading asks students to read a certain amount of text aloud, and, when finished, say another student's name. The student whose name is called is the next reader. After the second reader finishes reading, he/she repeats the process, calling on yet another student to be the reader. The process continues until the assigned section of reading is finished. Since popcorn reading traditionally relies on print-text literacies, one way to bring popcorn reading together with early reader comics or graphic novels is to ask students to read the print text along with the visual text. For example, let's consider what students may say aloud if they were asked to read a sequence from Lemony Snicket and Richard Sala's "It Was a Dark and Silly Night…" in *Big Fat Little Lit* (Puffin Books, 2006). In the first two panels of this particular story, early readers will read the text from the first panel ("In this case 'silly' stands for…Somewhat Intelligent Largely Laconic Yeti."), and then *read* the image ("An image of a snow monster is walking through the woods"). In the next panel, students will again read the text ("Lucretia had seen one outside the window, and heard it knock on the door") and the images ("An image of the snow monster is getting closer"). As each student takes his or her turn, he or she will place emphasis on reading the print text and the images, and, when finished, call upon the next reader to do the same. **IRA/NCTE standard alignment: Standards 1, 2, and 3**

Prediction	During predetermined stopping points in the text, ask students to predict what they think might happen next. Just like popcorn reading, the prediction reading strategy has traditionally focused on print-text literacies. To use prediction as a during-reading strategy with early reader comic books and graphic novels, you will need to stop at predetermined points in the story and ask students what will happen next in both the print text and the visual text. Ask students what the panels, gutters, and balloons have told them about the story so far and what they think will appear in upcoming panels, gutters, and balloons. **IRA/NCTE standard alignment: Standards 1, 2, and 3**
During-reading Reader's Theatre	Since students get a chance to get up and interact with their peers, reader's theatre is usually popular with early readers. And although reader's theatre typically serves as an after-reading strategy, it is a valuable during-reading strategy as well, especially when reading early reader comics and graphic novels. Break students into small groups, assign a portion of the text, and ask groups to both verbally and visually act out their assigned text in front of the class. Students will need to write a script that includes visual and verbal storytelling techniques. To visually depict panels, gutters, and balloons, students can use poster-sized paper (for panels) and smaller sheets of colored paper (for cutting out images and balloons to go in the panels). When the class is ready, each group will sequentially perform their reader's theatre. Aided by the reader's theatre performances and their own viewing of the text, students will have a stronger sense of comprehension. Note: Since reading the visual text is probably a new experience for most students, you may want to offer an example first. You may also want to point out that students have various options for depicting the visual text in their reader's theatre: • Deliberately act out the visual text, representing the specific details that the author has shown in his/her story. • Draw/create their own visual text, complementing the visual text from the story. • Make small, simple props to support the visual text from the story. **IRA/NCTE standard alignment: Standards 1, 2, and 3**

To help solidify comprehension upon the successful completion of a during-reading strategy, you will next choose an after-reading strategy. Figure 2.11 presents some after-reading strategies you can use.

FIGURE 2.11: **AFTER-READING STRATEGY OPTIONS FOR SECOND- AND THIRD-GRADE EARLY READER COMICS AND GRAPHIC NOVELS**

AFTER-READING STRATEGIES FOR SECOND- AND THIRD-GRADE READERS	EXPLANATION
Character Me	One way to engage students in reflecting on the story after they are finished reading is to ask them to consider themselves as a character in the story. Ask students: • If you were a character in this story, who would you be? Why? • What would you want to say to some of the other characters? Why? • If you could have magically jumped into the text at any point, where would you want to jump in at? Why? Note: After asking students these questions, you may want to engage them in a creative-writing activity as well, for this after-reading strategy easily lends itself to addressing the creative-writing standards. For example, offer copies of Appendix C to support student writing in the comic and graphic novel format with panels, gutters, and balloons. **IRA/NCTE standard alignment: Standards 1, 2, and 3. Standard 5 is addressed if you choose to add the writing activity.**

Reader's Theatre Rewrite	Ask students to think about what they would change if they were given a chance to rewrite the story. Briefly discuss their ideas. After this discussion, ask students to get into small groups, decide upon a rewrite idea for one part of the text, and then prepare a reader's theatre of that rewrite idea that makes use of panels, gutters, and balloons. To visually depict panels, gutters, and balloons, students can use poster-sized paper (for panels) and smaller sheets of colored paper (for cutting out images and balloons to go in the panels). Be sure to let students know that after each of their reader's theatre rewrite performances, the rest of the class will ask questions. In other words, make sure that students know that they will have to justify their rewrite decisions with evidence that links back to the original text. **IRA/NCTE standard alignment: Standards 1, 2, 3, and 5**
Visual Timeline	Draw a line on the board, leaving ample space both above and below the line. Ask students to think about significant events from the story. In individual panels, keep a list of these events on the board. Then, as a class, decide which five panels/events are most important to the storyline. Place each of the five events evenly along the line you drew earlier. To stress the visual aspect of reading comic books and graphic novels (like gutters and balloons), ask students to draw the same line (with the labeled events) on their own sheet of paper. Tell students that they now need to draw the images/balloons that best support each of the five events/panels. After students work on their own, ask for volunteers to draw one of their five visual representations on the board. You may want to have multiple representations for each of the five events. Multiple representations (or student responses) will foster greater discussion and, therefore, stronger comprehension of the text. Discuss the various image and balloon representations as a class. **IRA/NCTE standard alignment: Standards 1, 2, 3, and 5**

TEACHER RESOURCES FOR SECOND AND THIRD GRADE

This chapter's teacher resources for second and third grade include:

1. A comic book exposé of *Big Fat Little Lit*, edited by Art Spiegelman and Françoise Mouly (Figure 2.12).

2. An example guided-reading lesson plan that focuses on *Big Fat Little Lit* (Figure 2.13).

3. A blank guided-reading lesson plan for your classroom use (Figure 2.14).

FIGURE 2.12: **EARLY READER COMIC EXPOSÉ OF *BIG FAT LITTLE LIT***

Big Fat Little Lit, edited by Art Spiegelman and Françoise Mouly (Puffin Books, 2006)

Summary

A brilliant collection of leading children's authors and illustrators, *Big Fat Little Lit* offers young readers and their teachers a variety of comics from which to choose. From comics about silly nights to comics about being yourself (both inside and out) to comics that modernize traditional fables, fairy tales, and legends—and even a comic that allows the reader to choose his/her own visual reading adventure (think *Choose Your Own Adventure* with comics)—this collection has something for everyone.

Interesting information

A colleague summed it up perfectly: "Just a glimpse at the contributor list to *Big Fat Little Lit* made me want to teach this collection." Contributors include Maurice Sendak, Lemony Snicket, Art Spiegelman, Jules Feiffer, David Sedaris, Patrick McDonnell, and Neil Gaiman, just to name a few.

When asked to speak to readers of *Teaching Early Reader Comics and Graphic Novels*, Art Editor of *The New Yorker* and Co-editor of *Big Fat Little Lit* (alongside her Pulitzer-Prize-winning graphic novelist husband Art Spiegelman), Françoise Mouly shared the following thoughts on the importance of using comics and graphic novels with early readers:

> "Today's 'graphic novels' often aren't geared towards children. *Little Lit* addresses this gap with a collection of both brand-new and traditional tales that appeal to children of any age. For *Little Lit*, we called on some of the most renowned authors and artists of the children's books and literary world, including Ian Falconer, David Sedaris, Jules Feiffer, Neil Gaiman, Crockett Johnson, Harry Bliss, William Joyce, David Macauly, Barbara McClintock, Patrick McDonnell, J. Otto Seibold, Maurice Sendak, Lemony Snicket, and Art Spiegelman, among others. Contributors to *Big Fat Little Lit* have won and been nominated for nearly every award under the sun including the Caldecott Medal, Oscar®, Emmy Award, Grammy Award, Pulitzer Prize, Obie, and Golden Kite Award.
>
> It was important to us to include the masters of the past, such as Crockett Johnson (the author of *Harold and the Purple Crayon*), cheek-to-jowl with the cutting-edge wit of a David Sedaris. Sedaris wrote his kid-book story for Ian Falconer, the artist behind *Olivia*. Many years ago, Falconer had gotten his first break when I published his work on the

cover of *The New Yorker*. Wanting to introduce me to his friend, an unpublished writer who had was just started to do short pieces on the radio, he brought him to a *New Yorker* party. But Ian, his friend David Sedaris, and myself spent the whole party cooped up and laughing in my *New Yorker* office—it was the only place we could smoke. It wasn't until years later, after he had become hugely popular, that I was able to bring Sedaris into *The New Yorker*, and in *Little Lit*, I instigated a reunion between those two for the benefit of young children.

With such highly respected authors, *Little Lit* guarantees that children learn to love reading based on the quality of the stories. Even the most classic tales are told with a fresh twist, and the vibrant visuals keep young readers engaged. *Little Lit* encourages imagination by drawing children into the boundless universe of reading, filled with stories ranging from morbid to fantastic. The anthology amasses fairy tales, science fiction, mystery, and more into a collection that is clever, hilarious, and gripping.

Teachers and parents alike are finding that comics in general, and *Little Lit* in particular, can create a vital bridge between visually-based early readings and traditional literary culture. Professor James Bucky Carter, an assistant professor of English Education at the University of Texas at El Paso, has made use of *Big Fat Little Lit* in his university English courses. He asks students to use stories from the anthology to make connections with traditional works of literature, and their results point to the value of comics. Sedaris's "Pretty Ugly" is linked to *Paradise Lost*; it is suggested that Spiegelman's "The Several Selves of Shelby Sheldrake" bears a connection to *The Scarlet Letter*; and a fair few of the other *Little Lit* contributors garner references to Shakespeare. If the work of Professor Carter's classes is any indication, then the comics included in *Big Fat Little Lit* do far more than simply demonstrate to children that reading is enjoyable; they also establish a foundation of ethical and philosophical themes that are universal in the world's great literature. *Big Fat Little Lit* is meant to conserve the dynamic world of visual literacy for future generations of children, with the goal of helping to educate them and expand their horizons."

Besides being an amazing collection of comics by children's authors and illustrators, *Big Fat Little Lit* is often considered one of the best collections of early reader comics. For that reason, I would like to highlight some specific ways you can use *Big Fat Little Lit* in the classroom.

EXAMPLE GUIDED-READING LESSON PLAN FOR SECOND- AND THIRD-GRADE READERS	EXPLANATION
Before Reading	**Animated Schema** One of the most popular trends in children's literature and animation is the retelling and modernizing of traditional fables, fairy tales, and legends. Due to this popular trend, it might be wise to select a few of the comics from *Big Fat Little Lit* that retell some of these stories and introduce and build schema with them using an animated film clip that takes on the same premise. I recommend the following stories in particular: "It Was a Dark and Silly Night" by Lemony Snicket and Richard Sala, "The Princess and the Pea" by Barbara McClintock, "Cereal Baby Keller" by Maurice Sendak, "The Baker's Daughter" by Harry Bliss, "The Gingerbread Man" by Walt Kelly, and "A-Maze-ing Adventure" by Lewis Trondheim. The following is a list of animated films that have a retelling premise and are appropriate for second- and third-grade readers: • *Hoodwinked* • *Happily N'ever After* and *Happily N'ever After 2* • *Shrek, Shrek 2, Shrek the Third,* and *Shrek Forever After* **IRA/NCTE standard alignment: Standards 1, 2, and 3**

During Reading	**Prediction**
	
	Since many of the stories will be familiar to students, a during-reading prediction strategy often works well with the comics from *Big Fat Little Lit* that retell traditional stories.
	
	For this during-reading strategy, preview each of the comics and decide upon appropriate moments to stop the reading process and ask students to predict what might happen next.
	
	To reinforce the literary value of comics and graphic novels and the balance between print-text and visual literacies, provide students with some options from Appendix C, "iCreate Comics and Graphic Novels."
	
	At each stopping point, write down the following directions on the board.
	• On the "iCreate Comics and Graphic Novels" pages of your choice, use images and words to answer the following questions:
	    • What do you think the panels will show next?
	    • What do you think will happen in the gutters? To express your ideas about the gutters, please make writing notes/drawings in the margins between the panels.
	    • What might the upcoming word balloons say?
	
	After reading the entire comic, go back to students' predictions and discuss what they originally thought alongside with what really ended up happening.
	
	IRA/NCTE standard alignment: Standards 1, 2, and 3

After Reading	**What Comic Comes Next?** Use Appendix D, "What Comic Comes Next?," after reading *Big Fat Little Lit*. This appendix provides students with an opportunity to reflect on the significant events from each *Big Fat Little Lit* comic story. One *Big Fat Little Lit* comic at a time, ask students to think about significant events. Keep a list of all of their significant event ideas on the board. Then, in small groups, ask students to fill out "What Comic Comes Next?" This handout limits students to five panels; thus, each small group will need to ultimately decide what they think are the five most significant event ideas and put those ideas in the panels. Students can use words and/or images to represent their significant event decisions. To stress the importance of gutters and balloons as well, ask students to write notes in the gutters that explain why students chose the previous panel. Students can also draw balloons in order to add words. After students work on their own, ask for volunteers to share their work. Since the *Big Fat Little Lit* comic stories are short, it may also be a good idea to ask students to fill out more than one "What Comic Comes Next?" sheet as an after-reading strategy. **IRA/NCTE standard alignment: Standards 1, 2, 3, and 5**

For your teaching convenience, another blank guided-reading lesson plan is included on the following page (Figure 2.14).

GUIDED-READING LESSON PLAN FOR SECOND- AND FIRST-GRADE READERS	EXPLANATION
Before Reading	IRA/NCTE standard alignment: Standards 1, 2, and 3
During Reading	IRA/NCTE standard alignment: Standards 1, 2, and 3
After Reading	IRA/NCTE standard alignment: Standards 1, 2, 3, and 5

TEACHING EARLY READER COMICS AND GRAPHIC NOVELS TO STRIVING READERS

> **"With many young readers, there is a natural progression from reading with the visual reinforcement of picture books to being able to mentally visualize imageless text. But sometimes this transition happens more slowly. Comics and graphic novels provide an excellent bridge because they offer visual reinforcement like picture books while containing themes and vocabulary every bit as challenging as the chapter books targeted for their grade level."**
>
> *- Eric Wight, author of the Frankie Pickle series (Simon and Schuster) -*

One of my least favorite terms is *struggling readers*. However, this term is popularly used to refer to readers who have yet to discover their own passion for reading. I personally see these readers as *striving readers* who are on their way to reaching a goal, a goal that will allow them to not only enjoy reading, but also motivate them to keep reading. As reading teachers, it is our job to help striving readers reach these goals. And, just like Eric Wight mentioned above, sometimes these readers need their teachers to think a bit outside of the box in order to do so. This section aims to provide some new and hopefully exciting ideas for teaching early reader comics and graphic novels to *striving readers*.

Even when I feel as though I know a striving reader, I always approach him or her in the same way. It's a treasure hunt, and I am about to meet the unique individual who holds the treasure map in his or her hands. When emerging readers see themselves—and their own interests, motivations, schemas, and choices—as the treasure map, they tend to be more motivated to find the treasure.

Reading Engagement Theory (Guthrie and Wigfield, 1997) claims that there are four paths teachers should consider when engaging striving readers. The four paths are: Interest, Motivation, Choice, and Schema (Figure 2.15).

In essence, when teachers take Reading Engagement Theory into their classrooms, they have four key areas from which to generate questions. Figure 2.15 reworks the four areas of Reading Engagement Theory into four key questions teachers can ask their students.

QUESTIONS	ANSWERS
1. **Interest Question:** What are you interested in? Do you have any hobbies or activities that you would like to know more about?	
2. **Motivation Question:** What motivates or inspires you? In other words, what helps you to make a decision?	
3. **Choice Question:** If you could choose anything in the world to know more about, what would you choose?	
4. **Schema Question:** What books have you already read?	

Left blank for teacher use, the far right column of Figure 2.15 offers space for you to record student responses.

Armed with these responses, you can then make better and more informed decisions about each particular striving reader. To help further support your decision or general inkling about a striving reader, I also present the following even more detailed text-selection strategies (Figure 2.16). Linked directly to the four areas of Reading Engagement Theory, Figure 2.16 offers three text-selection strategies per category.

Schema Reading Strategies	*1.* **My Reading History** Similar to McKenna and Kear's work in *Measuring attitude toward reading: A new tool for teachers* (1990), this reading strategy seeks to discover a striving reader's previous reading experiences. With the lens of a historian, ask students the following questions: • Do you remember the first book you ever read or looked at? • When you were younger, what books do you remember seeing? Where did you see them? • Have you ever had a favorite book? • Previous to this school year, what have you read in school? What have you read at home or in a library? After students answer these questions, you can link what they now know about their students' schemas to appropriate grade-level comics and graphic novels. *2.* **Schema Stations** For this reading strategy, you will need to set up schema stations around the room, each with a large poster board and some markers. Each poster will be identified by one of the following schema-based ideas. For striving readers in kindergarten through third grade, I recommend three stations, each with a poster board labeled with one of the bulleted titles below. It is also recommended that the early reader teacher or teacher's aide(s) help students at each station. • Two books I have read • Two books I have at home • Two books my friends have read For striving readers in grades four through six, you can use the following three stations ideas. • Two books I have seen my parents, loved ones, or friends read • Two books I have seen and wanted to read at the library • Two books I have thought about asking my teacher to read at school When finished with the schema stations, collect and consult the poster boards to gain a better understanding of which early reader comics and graphic novels might best relate to their students' schema experiences. *3.* **Pin the Point on the Picture** This strategy gives striving readers a chance to nonverbally share their previous reading experiences. Choose pictures or clusters of pictures to display on the board that represent thematic story concepts that also relate to the IRA/NCTE standards. For example, if you want to teach the elements of story, such as setting, a cluster of pictures could show a forest, a house, an apartment, a store, etc. Supply each student with three check-mark symbols about three inches in height—with either sticky tape or a magnet on the back. Students place a check mark near pictures or clusters of pictures they feel they either already understand or want to know more about. Once students have placed their three check marks, you will have a better idea about which early reader comics and graphic novels to select and then build upon.

1. Category King

This strategy asks students to choose a category and then answer a question. The categories, prepared before class either for a board or a projected screen environment, should focus on appropriate grade-level themes. Sixth-grade teachers, for instance, may want to focus on themes relative to both the elements of story and their students' social studies curriculum: nineteenth-century American history, plot development, characters, facts and figures, the American Revolution, themes, battles, and so on.

Similar to the game show *Jeopardy*, each category should have about four or five questions. Unlike *Jeopardy*, however, the emphasis is not on points or money or winning a game. Instead, the emphasis is on having students share their ideas on topics they find motivating.

To get started, prepare the front of the question cards to be either visually or textually representative of a particular theme in your curriculum. If the category is the American Revolution, for example, the front of the card can either have that written out or visually represent the event with a relevant image like the "Join or Die" editorial logo popular at the time.

The flip side of the cards asks a question or displays an image that centers on exploring student motivation on that specific topic. In other words, instead of asking students for a "right" or "wrong" answer, the questions simply ask students to share how motivated they are to learn more about that topic. For example, if a student selects the card that says "The American Revolution," and finds a picture of George Washington on the back of the card, the motivation-oriented question could read something like: *If you could watch a video or read a book about George Washington and his role in the American Revolution, would you be motivated to learn more? Why or why not?* Another motivation question for the American Revolution category could read: *Would you be interested in learning more about the fact that the first national capital of America was not Washington D.C. but instead New York City?*

Once students have worked their way through the categories and the questions, you will have a better idea of which early reader comics and graphic novels will motivate your students.

Motivation Reading Strategies (cont'd.)	### 2. Decision Maker Prepare about 100–150 one-sided visual and/or verbal cue cards that focus on the topic or standard at hand. Place the cards face down and ask each student to select three cards. When turned face up, each card will have an image or a word/phrase that highlights the topic or standard you want to cover. The student's job is then to respond to the following prompt (displayed or projected for all students to see): *Turn your cards face up. Review each card and choose the one that you would be most motivated to learn more about. Be ready to share your ideas with the rest of the class.* In an effort to help students respond to the prompt, you may want to both state the question on the board and work your way around the classroom to talk to students about their motivation to choose one card over another card. To finalize this motivation strategy and better inform your comic or graphic novel choice, engage students in a whole-class discussion. ### 3. Inspiration Creation This motivation strategy is simple. Ask students to think about what inspires them. Ask questions like: • *How do you make a decision?* • *How do you choose a hero/someone to look up to?* • *What inspires you to do good?* • *Who motivates you to do your best work?* • *How do you know right from wrong?* It may be helpful to keep a list of student responses on the board.
Interest Reading Strategies	### 1. If I Could Read Anything… This interest-based strategy asks students to finish the statement: *If I could read anything, I would read….* After students write down their responses, engage them in a discussion, list ideas on the board, and use the list to select comics and graphic novels for class. ### 2. My Favorite Person, Place, or Thing Although traditional and familiar, this interest-based reading strategy is a staple and extremely helpful for selecting texts based on student interest. Simply write three categories on the board (*person*, *place*, and *thing*) and keep a list of student ideas to use for selecting appropriate comics and graphic novels. ### 3. Show and Tell with Reading Another traditional idea, this interest-based strategy asks students to not only show and tell, but also think very specifically about what they choose to show and tell. Instruct students to choose a book that they find very interesting and bring it to school for a "show and tell with reading." Students' choices will offer plenty of ideas for selecting comics and graphic novels.

Choice Reading Strategies

1. Choice Building Blocks

Give students two blank pieces of paper, each with one of the following labels: *Block 1* and *Block 2*. On each block, ask students to write in order of preference the title (block 1) or topic (block 2) of a book that they would choose to read. It may be beneficial to also allow students to draw images to represent their choices. When students are done writing or drawing on their blocks, collect them and use them to better inform your selection of comics and graphic novels.

2. My Dream Bookstore

Ask students to close their eyes and imagine their dream bookstore. With their eyes still closed, students should think about the following questions:

- *What types of books would your dream bookstore include?*
- *Of those books you just thought about, which would be on the top of your reading list?*

Once they have had enough thinking time, ask students to open their eyes and share their ideas with the class. Keep a running list of students' choices on the board, and use this list to inform your classroom reading selection.

3. Choice or Chance

You will need to prepare enough "choice" and "chance" cards so that there is one of each for every student in the class. The front of the cards will say either *choice* or *chance*, and the back of the cards will offer students options.

The choice cards should be broad, simply identifying a theme or instructional idea you see as critical to your curriculum. You will phrase that idea in the form of a question to students. For example, a choice card that stresses plot might read: *If you had to read a story with a great plot, what might that plot be about?*

Unlike the choice cards, the chance cards are more specific. Each chance card should contain an either/or scenario for students to choose from. A chance card focused on plot, for example, might read: *If you had to read a story about adventure or a story about science fiction, which would you choose?*

Each student decides whether to pick a "choice" or a "chance" card. Record student answers in a journal to aid in your selection of comics and graphic novels.

With students' interests, choices, motivations, and schemas more clearly understood and articulated, you can now select an appropriate early reader comic or graphic novel. Theme and grade-level suggestions can be found in the following cross-index.

Cross-index of Early Reader Comics and Graphic Novels by Theme and Grade Level

THEME

Title and Author	Act of Reading	Action-Adventure	Bravery	Coming of Age	Community	Culture	Diversity & Caring	Domestic Relations	Fairy Tales, Fables, & Folklore	Family	Fate, Destiny, and/or Chance	Foreign Relations	Friendship	Gender	Good & Evil	Heroes & Villains	Historical Context	Humanitarianism	Humor	Identity	Leadership	Loyalty & Trust	Myth & Legend	Narration	Plot Twists & Turns	Point of View	Relationships	School Life	Science Fiction	Space	Tradition	World Travel
Adventures in Cartooning by Sturm, Arnold, & Frederick-Frost	3-6	3-6							3-6							3-6			3-6				3-6	3-6	3-6							
Alia's Mission by Stamaty			3-6		3-6	3-6	3-6					3-6					3-6	3-6			3-6											
Amelia Rules! Superheroes by Gownley*		2-5	2-5	2-5									2-5	2-5		2-5			2-5	2-5							2-5	2-5				
Big Fat Little Lit, edited by Spiegelman & Mouly**	1-6	1-6	1-6	1-6	1-6	1-6	1-6		1-6	1-6	1-6		1-6	1-6	1-6	1-6	1-6		1-6	1-6		1-6	1-6		1-6		1-6	1-6	1-6			
Bone by Smith*		4-6	4-6	4-6	4-6				4-6		4-6	4-6			4-6	4-6	4-6		4-6	4-6		4-6	4-6		4-6		4-6					
Buddha by Tezuka*		4-6	4-6	4-6			4-6				4-6		4-6		4-6			4-6		4-6		4-6	4-6		4-6		4-6				4-6	
Buzzboy: Sidekicks Rule! by John Gallagher*																																
Dragonbreath by Vernon*		2-4	2-4								2-4		2-4						2-4	2-4	2-4				2-4		2-4	2-4	2-4			
Ed's Terrestrials by Sava & Jourdan		3-6	3-6		3-6		3-6						3-6	3-6		3-6		3-6	3-6						3-6		3-6		3-6	3-6		
Female Force by Bailey*	5-6		5-6	5-6	5-6	5-6	5-6			5-6			5-6	5-6			5-6			5-6	5-6											

Title and Author (cont'd.)	Act of Reading	Action-Adventure	Bravery	Coming of Age	Community	Culture	Diversity & Caring	Domestic Relations	Fairy Tales, Fables, & Folklore	Family	Fate, Destiny, and/or Chance	Foreign Relations	Friendship	Gender	Good & Evil	Heroes & Villains	Historical Context	Humanitarianism	Humor	Identity	Leadership	Loyalty & Trust	Myth & Legend	Narration	Plot Twists & Turns	Point of View	Relationships	School Life	Science Fiction	Space	Tradition	World Travel
Frankie Pickle and the Pine Run 3000 by Wight*	3-6	3-6	3-6		3-6						3-6		3-6						3-6	3-6	3-6				3-6		3-6					
Kaput & Zösky by Trondheim & Cartier*		3-6	3-6		3-6						3-6	3-6	3-6		3-6			3-6	3-6	3-6	3-6				3-6		3-6		3-6	3-6		
Knights of the Lunch Table: The Dodgeball Chronicles by Cammuso*		2-5	2-5		2-5					2-5			2-5		2-5				2-5	2-5	2-5		2-5		2-5		2-5	2-5				
Lex Luthor: Man of Steel by Azzarello & Bermejo		5-6	5-6					5-6			5-6					5-6	5-6			5-6					5-6							
Lockjaw and the Pet Avengers, published by Marvel*		3-6	3-6		3-6						3-6		3-6		3-6	3-6			3-6	3-6	3-6						3-6	3-6				
Luke on the Loose by Bliss		K-2			K-2	K-2	K-2			K-2									K-2	K-2												
Lunch Lady and the Cyborg Substitute by Krosoczka*		3-6	3-6		3-6								3-6		3-6				3-6	3-6	3-6				3-6		3-6					
Max Disaster #1: Alien Eraser to the Rescue by Moss*	2-4	2-4								2-4			2-4							2-4					2-4	2-4	2-4	2-4				
Middle School is Worse than Meatloaf by Holm & Castaldi	5-6			5-6						5-6			5-6							5-6								5-6				

Title and Author (cont'd.)	Act of Reading	Action-Adventure	Bravery	Coming of Age	Community	Culture	Diversity & Caring	Domestic Relations	Fairy Tales, Fables, & Folklore	Family	Fate, Destiny, and/or Chance	Foreign Relations	Friendship	Gender	Good & Evil	Heroes & Villains	Historical Context	Humanitarianism	Humor	Identity	Leadership	Loyalty & Trust	Myth & Legend	Narration	Plot Twists & Turns	Point of View	Relationships	School Life	Science Fiction	Space	Tradition	World Travel
Mo and Jo: Fighting Together Forever by Haspiel & Lynch*		K-3	K-3		K-3					K-3			K-3		K-3	K-3			K-3	K-3	K-3	K-3			K-3		K-3					
My Grandparents Are Secret Agents by Sava & Morgues		1-3	1-3							1-3					1-3	1-3			1-3	1-3		1-3	1-3		1-3		1-3					1-3
Nancy Drew, Girl Detective #1: The Demon of River Heights by Petrucha & Murase*			4-6	4-6							4-6		4-6	4-6	4-6	4-6					4-6				4-6							
Otto's Orange Day by Cammuso & Lynch		K-3		K-3	K-3					K-3								K-3		K-3					K-3							
Phonics Comics: Cave Dave—Level 1 by Moore & Dammer*	K-3	K-3																							K-3							
Phonics Comics: Clara the Klutz—Level 2 by Wax & Sullivan*	K-3	K-3																							K-3							
Phonics Comics: Duke and Fang—Level 3, by Katschke & Baumann*	K-3	K-3																							K-3							
Prime Baby by Yang				4-6			4-6			4-6	4-6				4-6			4-6	4-6	4-6							4-6	4-6				

THEME

Title and Author (cont'd.)	Act of Reading	Action-Adventure	Bravery	Coming of Age	Community	Culture	Diversity & Caring	Domestic Relations	Fairy Tales, Fables, & Folklore	Family	Fate, Destiny, and/or Chance	Foreign Relations	Friendship	Gender	Good & Evil	Heroes & Villains	Historical Context	Humanitarianism	Humor	Identity	Leadership	Loyalty & Trust	Myth & Legend	Narration	Plot Twists & Turns	Point of View	Relationships	School Life	Science Fiction	Space	Tradition	World Travel
Silly Lilly and the Four Seasons by Rosenstiehl		K-3		K-3															K-3	K-3				K-3								
Star Wars: Clone Wars Adventures, Volume 1, published by Dark Horse*		3-6	3-6	3-6			3-6			3-6	3-6	3-6	3-6		3-6			3-6		3-6	3-6	3-6	3-6		3-6	3-6			3-6	3-6		
Stink: The Incredible Shrinking Kid by McDonald & Reynolds				2-4						2-4			2-4						2-4	2-4					2-4		2-4	2-4				
Stinky by Davis			K-3		K-3		K-3						K-3					K-3				K-3					K-3					
Super Friends: Flying High, published by Random House and DC Comics*		K-3	K-3		K-3										K-3	K-3			K-3	K-3					K-3		K-3		K-3			
Superman: Red Son by Millar, Johnson, Plunkett, Robinson, & Wong*		5-6	5-6			5-6		5-6			5-6	5-6				5-6	5-6			5-6	5-6	5-6	5-6	5-6	5-6	5-6				5-6		
The Baby-Sitters Club: Kristy's Great Idea by Telgemeier*				2-5									2-5	2-5					2-5	2-5	2-5						2-5	2-5				
The Cryptics by Niles & Roman		2-4	2-4		2-4					2-4			2-4		2-4	2-4			2-4	2-4					2-4		2-4		2-4			

Title and Author (cont'd.)	Act of Reading	Action-Adventure	Bravery	Coming of Age	Community	Culture	Diversity & Caring	Domestic Relations	Fairy Tales, Fables, & Folklore	Family	Fate, Destiny, and/or Chance	Foreign Relations	Friendship	Gender	Good & Evil	Heroes & Villains	Historical Context	Humanitarianism	Humor	Identity	Leadership	Loyalty & Trust	Myth & Legend	Narration	Plot Twists & Turns	Point of View	Relationships	School Life	Science Fiction	Space	Tradition	World Travel
The Curse of the Bologna Sandwich (Melvin Beederman, Superhero) by Trine & Montijo*	K-2	K-2											K-2		K-2				K-2	K-2												
The Indispensable Calvin & Hobbes by Watterson*	2-6	2-6	2-6	2-6						2-6			2-6						2-6	2-6		2-6		2-6	2-6		2-6	2-6				
The Invention of Hugo Cabret by Selznick	5-6	5-6	5-6	5-6	5-6						5-6		5-6		5-6		5-6			5-6		5-6			5-6		5-6					5-6
The Revenge of the McNasty Brothers (Melvin Beederman, Superhero) by Trine & Montijo*	4-6	4-6	4-6		4-6					4-6			4-6			4-6			4-6	4-6	4-6				4-6		4-6					
The Toon Treasury of Children's Comics, edited by Spiegelman and Mouly	K-4	K-4		K-4	K-4		K-4						K-4		K-4		K-4		K-4	K-4		K-4	K-4				K-4				K-4	
Wolverine: Worst Day Ever by Lyga	3-6	3-6	3-6		3-6		3-6				3-6		3-6			3-6		3-6		3-6					3-6			3-6				

THEME

* This early reader comic or graphic novel is part of a series.

** This early reader comic or graphic novel has a diverse range of stories aimed at readers in grades 1-6.

Now that you have a better understanding of your students and the early reader comic or graphic novel you would like to teach, let's review the NCTE/IRA standards that best fit with using this genre to teach striving readers.

Standard 1
"Students read a wide range of print and non-print texts to build an understanding of texts, of themselves, and of the cultures of the United States and the world; to acquire new information; to respond to the needs and demands of society and the workplace; and for personal fulfillment. Among these texts are fiction and nonfiction, classic and contemporary works."

Standard 2
"Students read a wide range of literature from many periods in many genres to build an understanding of the many dimensions (e.g., philosophical, ethical, aesthetic) of human experience."

Standard 3
"Students apply a wide range of strategies to comprehend, interpret, evaluate, and appreciate texts. They draw on their prior experience, their interactions with other readers and writers, their knowledge of word meaning and of other texts, their word identification strategies, and their understanding of textual features (e.g., sound-letter correspondence, sentence structure, contexts, and graphics)."

With these three NCTE/IRA standards in mind and a selected comic or graphic novel in hand, you can now develop your lesson plans. I recommend using one of the following three grade-level, guided-reading lesson plans (Figures 2.17-2.19), each of which further reflects Reading Engagement Theory (Guthrie and Wigfield, 1997). Remember, these grade-level divisions are suggestions only, so you should choose lessons based on your students' abilities as well. You can also develop your own guided-reading lesson plans using the blank plan in Figure 2.20.

TEACHER RESOURCES FOR STRIVING READERS

This chapter's teacher resources for striving readers include:

1. An example guided-reading lesson plan that focuses on striving readers in kindergarten through second grade (Figure 2.17),

2. An example guided-reading lesson plan that focuses on striving readers in third and fourth grade (Figure 2.18),

3. An example guided-reading lesson plan that focuses on striving readers in fifth and sixth grade (Figure 2.19), and

4. A blank guided-reading lesson plan for your classroom use (Figure 2.20).

GUIDED-READING LESSON PLAN FOR STRIVING READERS IN KINDERGARTEN THROUGH SECOND GRADE	EXPLANATION
Before Reading	With the theme(s) of your early reader comic or graphic novel in mind, ask students what they know about that theme. Keep a list of student responses on the board. Instead of engaging students in a further discussion about this list, ask them to draw what they know. Let them know they can feel free to draw either their own ideas or the ideas of their peers. Finally, call on students to discuss their drawings. What did they decide to draw? And why? **IRA/NCTE standard alignment: Standards 1, 2, and 3**
During Reading	To follow up on your before-reading discussion, ask students to continue to draw their responses to what they are reading. Take notes on the board again. Discuss students' reading notes and drawings as you move through the text. Make multiple copies of Appendix C to use for these during-reading drawings. **IRA/NCTE standard alignment: Standards 1, 2, and 3**
After Reading	After students read the entire comic or graphic novel, ask them to reflect upon the major themes. Keep a list of these themes on the board. Then, with these themes in mind, ask students to get into small groups and select one theme. With their chosen theme in mind, students can write a multiple-page comic or graphic novel story of their choice. Feel free to offer students multiple pages or copies of Appendix C, "iCreate Comics and Graphic Novels," to help with their writing ideas. When students are finished, they can share their stories with the class. **IRA/NCTE standard alignment: Standards 1, 2, and 3**

FIGURE 2.18: SUGGESTED GUIDED-READING LESSON PLAN FOR TEACHING EARLY READER COMICS AND GRAPHIC NOVELS TO STRIVING READERS IN GRADES THREE AND FOUR

GUIDED-READING LESSON PLAN FOR STRIVING READERS IN GRADES THREE AND FOUR	EXPLANATION
Before Reading	Select a variety of elements of story from your chosen comic or graphic novel: character(s), setting(s), plot(s), theme(s), and so on. Find a visual representation for each of your choices (preferably standard paper size of 8½ " x 11"), and post those visuals in the front of the room. Similar to the "pin the point on the picture" text selection strategy mentioned earlier in this chapter, prepare and hand out two 3"x5" check marks to each student. Ask students to place their check marks on the visual they would like to learn more about. Once all check marks are placed on the board, and in an effort to build student schema toward the selected comic or graphic novel, call on students to explain their placements. **IRA/NCTE standard alignment: Standards 1, 2, and 3**
During Reading	As students begin to read, I recommend that you connect the visual elements of story to the verbal labels for those elements, thus further emphasizing IRA/NCTE standards 1-3 with verbal and visual literacies. In order to do so, choose and prepare the elements of story to display on the board, and create a handout that both labels and visually represents those elements. Have students complete the handout and engage in discussion for each assigned reading. **IRA/NCTE standard alignment: Standards 1, 2, and 3**
After Reading	When students are done reading the comic or graphic novel, ask them to reflect upon all of their handouts collectively. The prompts for this reflection can be put on the board: 1. *With a peer, re-read and reflect on the elements of story found on your handouts.* 2. *Choose one of the elements of story that you think is most influential to the story.* 3. *In your opinion, why is this element of story so significant?* Record and discuss student responses. **IRA/NCTE standard alignment: Standards 1, 2, and 3**

GUIDED-READING LESSON PLAN FOR STRIVING READERS IN GRADES FIVE AND SIX	EXPLANATION
Before Reading	To start, pre-select interesting panels, gutter sequences, and balloons from the text and make a copy of each. Depending upon how many students are in your classroom, you will want to make sure you have at least two selections per student. Once they are selected and copied, fold the paper they are printed on into a small square. Place these folded copies in a container in the front of the room and ask students to individually come up and, without looking, make two selections. Once they have two selections in hand, students can return to their seats and be asked to leaf through the comic or graphic novel the class will be reading and, with their two choices in mind, decide upon which one they would like to learn more about as they read. **IRA/NCTE standard alignment: Standards 1, 2, and 3**
During Reading	While students read the comic or graphic novel, their job is now to not only find the exact panel, gutter sequence, or balloon they selected, but also be cognizant of how that panel, gutter sequence, or balloon relates to and influences the entire story. Write a prompt instructing students to do so on the board. **IRA/NCTE standard alignment: Standards 1, 2, and 3**
After Reading	When students finish the comic or graphic novel, ask them to write a short paragraph that identifies the location of their selection and explains the overall significance of their selection in both its specific location and within the story as a whole. **IRA/NCTE standard alignment: Standards 1, 2, and 3**

GUIDED-READING LESSON PLAN FOR STRIVING READERS IN GRADES _____	EXPLANATION
Before Reading	IRA/NCTE standard alignment: Standards 1, 2, and 3
During Reading	IRA/NCTE standard alignment: Standards 1, 2, and 3
After Reading	IRA/NCTE standard alignment: Standards 1, 2, and 3

-CHAPTER 3-

TEACHING EARLY READER COMICS AND GRAPHIC NOVELS TO ADVANCED READERS

"This bridge will only take you halfway there, to those mysterious lands you long to see. Through Gypsy camps and swirling Arab fair, and moonlit woods where unicorns run free. So come and walk awhile with me and share the twisting trails and wondrous worlds I've known. But this bridge will only take you halfway there. The last few steps you have to take alone."

- Shel Silverstein -

Many of the state standards for teaching language arts in fourth through sixth grade ask teachers to examine—in detail—the reciprocal relationship that exists between reading and writing. As a result, this chapter will place a stronger emphasis on teaching students to not only read early reader comics and graphic novels, but also write them.

The following grab bag (Figure 3.1) presents some of the best early reader comics and graphic novels on the market for fourth- through sixth-grade students. Again, the grade levels are suggestions only, any many of these titles appeal to advanced readers in earlier grades. Check http://teachinggraphicnovels.blogspot.com for continuous, up-to-date announcements of newly published comics and graphic novels.

American Born Chinese by Gene Luen Yang (Square Fish, 2006)
Amulet by Kazu Kibuishi (GRAPHIX, 2008)*
Artemis Fowl: The Graphic Novel, adapted by Eoin Colfer and Andrew Donkin (Hyperion, 2007)*
Astronaut Academy by Dave Roman (First Second, 2011)
Bone: Quest for the Spark by Jeff Smith and Tom Sniegoski (GRAPHIX, 2011)*
Bone: Tall Tales by Jeff Smith and Tom Sniegoski (GRAPHIX, 2010)*
Booth by C.C. Colbert and Tanitoc (First Second, 2010)
Buzzboy: Sidekicks Rule! by John Gallagher (Sky-Dog Comics, 2007)*
Daisy Kutter: The Last Train by Kazu Kibuishi (Viper Comics, 2006)
Daniel X: Alien Hunter by James Patterson and Leopoldo Gout (Little, Brown, 2008)*
Diary of a Wimpy Kid, Jeff Kinney (Amulet Books, 2007)*
Flink by Doug TenNapel (Image Comics, 2007)
Foiled by Jane Yolen and Mike Cavallaro (First Second, 2010)*
Four Eyes by Joe Kelly (Image Comics, 2010)*
Gettysburg: The Graphic Novel by C..M. Butzer (HarperCollins, 2009)
Ghostopolis by Doug TenNapel (GRAPHIX, 2010)
Gods of Asgard by Erik Evensen (Studio E3, 2007)
Mary Shelley's Frankenstein, published by Campfire (2010)**
Middle School Is Worse Than Meatloaf by Jennifer Holms and Elicia Castaldi (Simon & Schuster, 2007)
Missile Mouse by Jake Parker (GRAPHIX, 2010)*
Prince of Persia: The Graphic Novel by Jordan Michner, A.B. Sina, LeUyen Pham, and Alex Puvilland (First Second, 2010)
Resistance: Book 1 by Carla Jablonski and Leland Purvis (First Second, 2010)*
Spiral-Bound by Aaron Renier (Top Shelf Productions, 2005)
Smile by Raina Telgemeier (GRAPHIX, 2010)
Superman: Birthright by Mark Waid, Leinil Francis Yu, and Gerry Alanguilan (DC Comics, 2004)*
Superman: Red Son by Mark Millar (DC Comics, 2003)
The Adventures of Digger and Friends, published by IDW (2010)
The Baby-Sitters Club: Kristy's Great Idea by Raina Telgemeier (GRAPHIX, 2006)*
The Demon of River Heights (Nancy Drew, Girl Detective #1) by Stefan Petrucha and Sho Murase (Papercutz, 2006)*
The Invention of Hugo Cabret by Brian Selznick (Scholastic Press, 2007)
The Meaning of Life...and Other Stuff by Jimmy Gownley (Atheneum, 2011)*
The Quest of Perseus by Paul Collins, illustrated by Chris Burns (Educators Publishing Service, 2008)**
Tommysaurus Rex by Doug TenNapel (Image Comics, 2005)
Top Ten Deadliest Sharks by Discovery Channel (Zenescope, 2010)
Wolverine: Worst Day Ever by Barry Lyga (Marvel Books, 2009)
Your Life in Comics: 100 Things for Guys to Write and Draw by Bill Zimmerman (Free Spirit Publishing, 2010)
Zita the Spacegirl by Ben Hatke (First Second, 2011)

* This graphic novel is part of a series.
**This publisher offers more than this one graphic novel adaptation of a literary classic.

Fortunately, eight of the twelve IRA/NCTE standards can be aligned to teaching fourth-through sixth-grade early reader comics and graphic novels:

Standard 1
"Students read a wide range of print and non-print texts to build an understanding of texts, of themselves, and of the cultures of the United States and the world."

Standard 2
"Students read a wide range of literature from many periods in many genres to build an understanding of the many dimensions (e.g., philosophical, ethical, aesthetic) of human experience."

Standard 3
"Students apply a wide range of strategies to comprehend, interpret, evaluate, and appreciate texts. They draw on their prior experience, their interactions with other readers and writers, their knowledge of word meaning and of other texts, their word identification strategies, and their understanding of textual features."

Standard 4
"Students adjust their use of spoken, written, and visual language (e.g., conventions, style, vocabulary) to communicate effectively with a variety of audiences and for different purposes."

Standard 5
"Students employ a wide range of strategies as they write and use different writing process elements appropriately to communicate with different audiences for a variety of purposes."

Standard 6
"Students apply knowledge of language structure, language conventions (e.g., spelling and punctuation), media techniques, figurative language, and genre to create, critique, and discuss print and non-print texts."

Standard 11
"Students participate as knowledgeable, reflective, creative, and critical members of a variety of literacy communities."

Standard 12
"Students use spoken, written, and visual language to accomplish their own purposes (e.g., for learning, enjoyment, persuasion, and the exchange of information)."

Since these eight IRA/NCTE standards focus on reading and writing, this chapter will present both a model guided-reading lesson plan and a model guided-writing lesson plan. Both of these lesson plan examples will focus on children's author Jane Yolen and her first graphic novel, *Foiled* (2010), illustrated by Mike Cavallaro.

Before taking a look at *Foiled*, however, you should decide which set of comic and graphic novel terms—basic or advanced—you would like to introduce to students (found in Appendix A and Appendix B).

TEACHER RESOURCES FOR FOURTH THROUGH SIXTH GRADE

This chapter's teacher resources for fourth through sixth grade include:

1. A comic book exposé of Jane Yolen's *Foiled* (Figure 3.2),

2. An example guided-reading lesson plan that focuses on *Foiled* (Figure 3.3),

3. An example guided-writing lesson plan that focuses on *Foiled* (Figure 3.4),

4. A blank guided-reading lesson plan for your classroom use (Figure 3.5), and

5. A blank guided-writing lesson plan for your classroom use (Figure 3.6).

FIGURE 3.2: **EARLY READER GRAPHIC NOVEL EXPOSÉ OF *FOILED***

Foiled, written by Jane Yolen and illustrated by Mike Cavallaro (First Second, 2010)

Summary
Aliera Carstairs doesn't know where she belongs. She's invisible at school. She's too visible at practice. Fencing practice, that is.

A teenage prodigy headed for a national-level fencing competition, Aliera is capable of beating both teenage challengers her own age and college challengers with more experience. But none of that seems to matter to anyone at school. That is, until she's paired with "Prince Charming" himself as a science lab partner: Avery Castle. Almost magically, Aliera is no longer invisible at school.

At the end of the day, however, Aliera must leave her newfound school visibility and head off to her superstar visibility at fencing practice. When she gets there, she recalls her coach's early advice: "It's all about protecting the heart, Aliera. You must always protect your heart."

Accompanied by Mike Cavallaro's swift and engaging illustrations, Jane Yolen's Aliera must realize the power behind being both visible and invisible and how, no matter what, she can protect her heart.

Yolen and Cavallaro's *Foiled*, in short, presents an assortment of engaging reading and writing topics to choose from: identity, school vs. family life, relationships, and social status, just to name a few. With these rich teaching topics to choose from and all eight of the IRA/NCTE standards in mind, I present a model guided-reading lesson plan and a model guided-writing lesson plan.

Interesting information
Jane Yolen is the author of the graphic novels *Foiled* (First Second), *Curses, Foiled Again* (First

Second), and *The Last Dragon* (Dark Horse Comics), as well as *Owl Moon* (Philomel), *How Do Dinosaurs Say Goodnight?* (Scholastic), *The Devil's Arithmetic* (Penguin), and 300 other books.

Mike Carallaro is a writer, an illustrator, and an artist. Along with *Foiled*, you can find more of Mike's brilliantly smooth and alluring style in some of his other works: *Parade (with Fireworks)* (Image Comics), *Act-i-Vate Primer* (Idea & Design Works), *Life and Times of Savoir* 28 #2 and #5 (IDW Publishing), and, finally, *Secret Weapons #1* (Valiant Comics).

When asked to speak to readers of *Teaching Early Reader Comics and Graphic Novels*, Jane Yolen wanted to reach out to both teachers and students:

> For teachers: "I believe in sentence structure and story. I believe in glorious words, and characters who hop off the page and burrow into the reader's heart. And the best of graphic novels can give that to the reader, too."

> For students: "It's amazing what true life adventures a writer can use to begin a story. I lost my fencing foil way back in the early 1960s on a date in Grand Central Station. No, I have no memory of who I was dating or why I had my foil with me or how it got lost. However, to answer that long nagging question (and to share a moment with my granddaughter Maddison who was then a young fencer), I started *Foiled*. It took on its own life, as a book will. I hope it will become part of your lives, too."

From an artist's perspective, Mike Cavallaro said he hopes early reader comics and graphic novels encourage students to tell their own stories:

> "Comics can be about anything. They're a *way* of telling a story, *any* story, not just a certain *type* of story. The best thing a comic creator can do is to tell us stories *only they can tell*. Whether it's based on fact or fiction, give it some personal truth that makes the story unique and essential."

GUIDED-READING LESSON PLAN FOR FOURTH- THROUGH SIXTH-GRADE STUDENTS	EXPLANATION
Before Reading	**Schema Brainstorming** Thinking of the school setting in *Foiled*, students should brainstorm what they think might happen in a graphic novel set in a school. Next, tell students that, along with a focus on a school setting, *Foiled* is also about a young girl whose sport is fencing. Ask students what they know about fencing. To help students generate both verbal and visual ideas, you may want to offer students some comic and graphic novel drafting pages (found in Appendix C). Keep a list of both types of student responses—with words and images—on the board. **IRA/NCTE standard alignment: Standards 1, 2, and 3**
During Reading	**Quick-draw Predictions** For this during-reading strategy, choose some comfortable places to stop and ask for "quick-draw" predictions. A quick-draw prediction is when students stop reading and have only a couple of minutes to draw what they think might happen next in the story. Supply a selection of comic and graphic novel pages (found in Appendix C) and a few drawing/coloring supplies so that students can put their predictions in the blank panels, gutters, and word balloons. After students have completed each quick draw, allow time for sharing and class discussion. **IRA/NCTE standard alignment: Standards 1, 2, and 3**

After Reading	**Alternate Endings** Since the ending of *Foiled* is so engaging and rich with classroom discussion points, keep the drawing and coloring supplies nearby, as well as a solid supply of comic and graphic novel drafting pages (Appendix C). Ask students to create alternate endings for *Foiled*. Performing a simple Google image search for "comic panel worksheets" will garner more drafting page options to choose from. I also recommend the following teacher-friendly websites and books: • www.comicsintheclassroom.net • http://www.comicbookproject.org/ • http://www.toon-books.com/classroom.php • http://www.professorgarfield.org/pgf_Intro.html • http://www.graphicclassroom.blogspot.com • *Building Literacy Connections with Graphic Novels*, edited by James Bucky Carter (NCTE, 2007) • *Super-Powered Word Study* by James Bucky Carter and Erik Evensen (Maupin House, 2010) • *Making Comics* by Scott McCloud (Harper, 2006) • *Your Life in Comics* by Bill Zimmerman (Free Spirit, 2010) • *When Commas Meet Kryptonite* by Michael Bitz (Teachers College Press, 2010) • *Teaching Graphic Novels* by Katie Monnin (Maupin House, 2010) When students have completed their alternate endings, I also suggest allowing time for class discussion. These discussions are important because, according to the NCTE/IRA standards, students need to be able to connect their own, creative ideas to aspects of the story that supported such interpretations. **IRA/NCTE standard alignment: Standards 4, 5, 6, 11, and 12**

Once students have successfully worked through a guided-reading lesson plan, they are ready to think about becoming writers of comics and graphic novels. To start this process, ask students to think about how the words and the images from *Foiled* work together to tell the story.

Next, place students in small groups and transition into the guided-writing lesson plan (Figure 3.4).

GUIDED-WRITING LESSON PLAN FOR FOURTH- THROUGH SIXTH-GRADE STUDENTS	EXPLANATION
Plan	Since the guided-reading lesson plan for *Foiled* concluded with alternate endings, you can prepare a guided-writing lesson plan that builds upon that idea. To begin, students should be organized into groups of three or four (which can be divided by ability level, by putting strong and striving writers together, or randomly). Even though students will write as individuals, this group setting will help them encourage each other's writing ideas. Be sure students have comic book- or graphic novel-friendly paper (copies of Appendix C), writing and drawing utensils, coloring supplies, and extra scratch paper. **IRA/NCTE standard alignment: Standards 4, 5, 6, 11, and 12**
Mini-lesson	Begin the mini-lesson by writing the word *series* on the board. Students can write the word *series* in their notes as well. Then, define the word as a class, with students keeping notes as the discussion progresses. Next, ask students if they know any other stories that are part of a series. You may want to bring in some examples for student perusal as well. Once they understand the word *series* and are familiar with some other examples, ask students to re-read the alternate endings they wrote after reading *Foiled*. This is also a good time to share that Jane Yolen and Make Cavallaro are planning to continue writing *Foiled* as a series. Thus, with their alternate endings in mind, and the knowledge that *Foiled* is indeed going to become a series, students should think about how their own ideas might inform the next *Foiled* graphic novel. Ask students: "If you could help Jane Yolen and Mike Cavallaro write the next *Foiled* graphic novel, what would you want to say to them?" Encourage students to actually write—with words and with images—a possible story idea for the next *Foiled* graphic novel. To support this, make a variety of some of the blank comic and graphic novel handouts from Appendix C available and ask students to use both words and images to show Yolen and Cavallaro *exactly* what they think should happen next in the *Foiled* series. **IRA/NCTE standard alignment: Standards 4, 5, 6, 11, and 12**

Write	Students write out their own series ideas using the blank comic and graphic novel pages of their choice (Appendix C).
Conference	Move from group to group and conference with students as they write. Specifically, make sure that students are writing using the comic/graphic novel format of words and images.
Share	For the last step in this guided-writing lesson plan, engage in an open, whole-class discussion about students' series ideas for *Foiled*. If possible, display students' ideas on a projector for the whole class to see. This will help the entire class better understand all of the various ways in which their peers have made use of panels, gutters, and balloons—and it's fun to see what ideas everyone came up with. **IRA/NCTE standard alignment: Standards 4, 5, 6, 11, and 12**

Figures 3.5 and 3.6 offer blank, copy-friendly, guided-reading and guided-writing lesson plans for your own creative, inspiring teaching ideas with early reader comics and graphic novels.

FIGURE 3.5: BLANK, COPY-FRIENDLY GUIDED-READING LESSON PLAN FOR TEACHERS OF FOURTH- THROUGH SIXTH-GRADE STUDENTS

GUIDED-READING LESSON PLAN FOR FOURTH- THROUGH SIXTH-GRADE STUDENTS	EXPLANATION
Before Reading	
During Reading	
After Reading	

FIGURE 3.6: **BLANK, COPY-FRIENDLY GUIDED-WRITING LESSON PLAN FOR TEACHERS OF FOURTH- THROUGH SIXTH-GRADE STUDENTS**

GUIDED-WRITING LESSON PLAN FOR FOURTH- THROUGH SIXTH-GRADE STUDENTS	EXPLANATION
Plan	
Mini-lesson	
Write	
Conference	
Share	

If you would like to share your own guided-reading and guided-writing lesson plans, please do so at http://teachinggraphicnovels.blogspot.com.

-CHAPTER 4-
TEACHING MULTICULTURAL EARLY READER COMICS AND GRAPHIC NOVELS

> "The more that you read, the more things you will know.
> The more that you learn, the more places you'll go."
>
> *- Dr. Seuss -*

One of the greatest areas of need in regards to early reader comics and graphic novels is the need for more multicultural texts. A sad reality. Period.

Because comics and graphic novels rely on readers to be competent readers of both textual literacies and visual literacies, both types of literacy are equally powerful. It's like a superhero team with each team member contributing his or her own unique ability to solve problems and generate meaning. Readers of multicultural early reader comics and graphic novels are presented with two opportunities—print text and image text—through which they may learn about and mature in regard to diverse people and diverse ideas. Thus, the lack of diverse, multicultural early reader comics and graphic novels presents a problem for teachers who wish to teach *for* and *to* all people. I hope this chapter begins a conversation that calls on the early reader comic and graphic novel community to place more focus on diverse ideas and people while also—and more importantly, in regard to the scope of this book—identifying and uniting teachers with the high-quality early reader comics and graphic novels that are indeed out there.

When you teach comics and graphic novels, cultural subject matter needs to be responsibly represented both textually and visually. To help early reader teachers select responsible and multiculturally representative early reader comics and graphic novels, I developed the following checklist (Figure 4.1).

	THIS EARLY READER COMIC OR GRAPHIC NOVEL'S TEXT AND IMAGES
	Avoid stereotyping
	Include significant and relative historical events
	Are not derogatory
	Encourage positive, harmonious relationships
	Respect its subject matter
	Foster culturally diverse thinking
	Have earned positive attention from reputable educational sources
	Enhance student understanding of various people and cultures

This checklist is intended to promote a broad definition of multicultural literature while helping teachers select socially just and varied multicultural literature that will positively inform how early readers think about diversity—both textually and visually.

With these characteristics of high-quality, responsible multicultural literature in mind, Figure 4.2 presents a grade-level list of some of the best early reader comics and graphic novels on the market.

FIGURE 4.2: **MULTICULTURAL COMIC BOOK AND GRAPHIC NOVEL GRADE-LEVEL GRAB BAG**

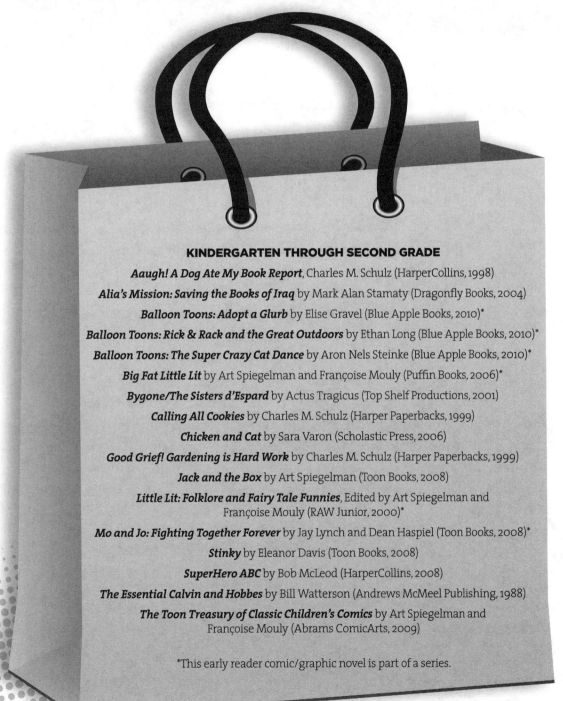

KINDERGARTEN THROUGH SECOND GRADE

Aaugh! A Dog Ate My Book Report, Charles M. Schulz (HarperCollins, 1998)

Alia's Mission: Saving the Books of Iraq by Mark Alan Stamaty (Dragonfly Books, 2004)

Balloon Toons: Adopt a Glurb by Elise Gravel (Blue Apple Books, 2010)*

Balloon Toons: Rick & Rack and the Great Outdoors by Ethan Long (Blue Apple Books, 2010)*

Balloon Toons: The Super Crazy Cat Dance by Aron Nels Steinke (Blue Apple Books, 2010)*

Big Fat Little Lit by Art Spiegelman and Françoise Mouly (Puffin Books, 2006)*

Bygone/The Sisters d'Espard by Actus Tragicus (Top Shelf Productions, 2001)

Calling All Cookies by Charles M. Schulz (Harper Paperbacks, 1999)

Chicken and Cat by Sara Varon (Scholastic Press, 2006)

Good Grief! Gardening is Hard Work by Charles M. Schulz (Harper Paperbacks, 1999)

Jack and the Box by Art Spiegelman (Toon Books, 2008)

Little Lit: Folklore and Fairy Tale Funnies, Edited by Art Spiegelman and Françoise Mouly (RAW Junior, 2000)*

Mo and Jo: Fighting Together Forever by Jay Lynch and Dean Haspiel (Toon Books, 2008)*

Stinky by Eleanor Davis (Toon Books, 2008)

SuperHero ABC by Bob McLeod (HarperCollins, 2008)

The Essential Calvin and Hobbes by Bill Watterson (Andrews McMeel Publishing, 1988)

The Toon Treasury of Classic Children's Comics by Art Spiegelman and Françoise Mouly (Abrams ComicArts, 2009)

*This early reader comic/graphic novel is part of a series.

GRADES THREE AND FOUR

Adventures in Cartooning by James Sturm, Andrew Arnold, and Alexis Frederick-Frost (First Second, 2009)

Adventures in Cartooning: Activity Book by James Sturm, Andrew Arnold, and Alexis Frederick-Frost (First Second, 2010)

Bone: Out from Boneville by Jeff Smith (Scholastic, 2005)*

Buddha by Osamu Tezuka (Vertical, 2006)*

Cryptics by Steve Niles and Benjamin Roman (IDW Publishing, 2008)*

Ed's Terrestrials by Scott Christian Sava and Diego Jourdan (Idea & Design Works, 2008)

Fang Fairy by Andy Smith (Stone Arch Books, 2007)*

Frankie Pickle and the Pine Run 3000 by Eric Wight (Simon & Schuster, 2010)*

Jellaby by Kean Soo (Hyperion, 2008)*

Laika by Nick Abadzis (First Second, 2007)

Little Vampire by Joann Sfar (First Second, 2008)

Lunch Lady and the Cyborg Substitute by Jarrett Krosoczka (Knopf, 2009)*

Kaput and Zösky by Lewis Trondheim, with Eric Cartier (First Second, 2002)*

Mama's Boyz: Home Schoolin' by Jerry Craft (Mama's Boyz, Inc., 2007)*

Meanwhile: Pick Any Path. 3,856 Story Possibilities by Jason Shiga (Amulet Books, 2010)

My Grandparents Are Secret Agents by Scott Christian Sava and Juan Saavedra Mourgues (Idea & Design Works, 2009)

Otto's Orange Day by Frank Cammuso and Jay Lynch (Toon Books, 2010)

Sardine in Outer Space by Emmanuel Guibert and Joann Sfar (First Second, 2006)*

Satchel Paige by James Sturm and Rich Tommaso (Hyperion, 2007)

Star Wars: Clone Wars Adventures, Volume 1, published by Dark Horse Comics (Dark Horse, 2004)*

Tiny Tyrant by Lewis Trondheim and Fabrice Parme (First Second, 2007)

*This early reader comic/graphic novel is part of a series.

GRADES FIVE AND UP

Amelia Rules! Superheroes by Jimmy Gownley (Renaissance Press, 2006)*

American Born Chinese by Gene Luen Yang (Square Fish, 2008)

Buzzboy: Sidekicks Rule! by John Gallagher (Sky-Dog Comics, 2007)*

Castle Waiting by Linda Medley (Fantagraphics Books, 2006)

Chiggers by Hope Larson (Aladdin, 2008)

Crogan's Vengeance by Chris Schweizer (Oni Press, 2008)*

Deogratias: A Tale of Rwanda by Stassen, translated by Alexis Siegel (First Second, 2006)

Diary of a Wimpy Kid by Jeff Kinney (Amulet Books, 2007)*

Earthboy Jacobus by Doug TenNapel (Image Comics, 2005)

Female Force by Neal Bailey (Bluewater Productions, 2009)*

Forget Sorrow by Belle Yang (W. W. Norton & Company, 2010)

Journey into Mohawk Country by Harmen Meyndertsz van den Bogaert and George O'Connor (First Second, 2006)

King: The Special Edition by Ho Che Anderson (Fantagraphics Books, 2010)

Knights of the Lunch Table: The Dodgeball Chronicles by Frank Cammuso (GRAPHIX, 2008)*

The Lost Colony, Book One: The Snodgrass Conspiracy by Grady Klein (First Second, 2006)*

Mouse Guard: Fall 1152 by David Petersen (Archaia Studios Press, 2007)*

Resistance: Book 1 by Carla Jablonski and Leland Purvis (First Second, 2010)*

Spiral-Bound by Aaron Renier (Top Shelf Productions, 2005)

Still I Rise: A Graphic History of African Americans by Roland Laird, with Taneshia Nash Laird, illustrated by Elihu "Adofo" Bey (Sterling, 2009)

Superman: Red Son by Mark Millar, Dave Johnson, Kilian Plunkett, Andrew Robinson, and Walden Wong (DC Comics, 2004)*

Superman: Secret Identity by Kurt Busiek and Stuart Immonen (Titan Books, 2005)*

Trickster: Native American Tales: A Graphic Collection by Matt Dembicki (Fulcrum Publishing, 2010)

The Unsinkable Walker Bean by Aaron Renier (First Second, 2010)

*This early reader comic/graphic novel is part of a series.

Whenever I teach multicultural early reader comics and graphic novels, I like to cite one of my favorite movies. The primary theme behind Disney/Pixar's *UP* is "Adventure is out there!" "Adventure is out there!" not only builds excitement about other people, cultures, and ideas, but also applies to the IRA/NCTE standards for teaching multicultural literature.

The most applicable IRA/NCTE standards for multicultural early reader comics and graphic novels are standard 1, 9, 10, and 11.

Standard 1

"Students read a wide range of print and non-print texts to build an understanding of texts, of themselves, and of the cultures of the United States and the world; to acquire new information; to respond to the needs and demands of society and the workplace; and for personal fulfillment. Among these texts are fiction and nonfiction, classic and contemporary works."

Standard 9

"Students develop an understanding of and respect for diversity in language use, patterns, and dialects across cultures, ethnic groups, geographic regions, and social roles."

Standard 10

"Students whose first language is not English make use of their first language to develop competency in the English language arts and to develop understanding of content across the curriculum."

Standard 11

"Students participate as knowledgeable, reflective, creative, and critical members of a variety of literacy communities."

Before teachers develop their lesson plans with these standards in focus, however, and just like in the earlier chapters, teachers need to introduce students to Appendix A and Appendix B. Again, it is imperative that students be acquainted with either the basic or advanced terminology for reading comics and graphic novels. The choice between basic or advanced is up to you, the teacher, and your knowledge of your students.

With either the basic or the advanced terminology understood, teachers are ready to introduce students to the lesson plans that will link one (or more) of the IRA/NCTE multicultural standards to the selected early reader comic or graphic novel. Since this chapter's focus is on multicultural early reader comics and graphic novels, I suggest that teachers embrace the "Adventure is out there!" theme. And adventure is certainly out there when students embark on a multicultural reading journey with comics and graphic novels.

Figures 4.3 (written for teachers of kindergarten through second grade) and 4.4 (written for third- through sixth-grade teachers) each explain the "Adventures is out there!" theme and how teachers can use it to embrace multicultural early reader comics and graphic novels.

TEACHER RESOURCES FOR USING MULTICULTURAL EARLY READER COMICS AND GRAPHIC NOVELS

This chapter's teacher resources for using multicultural early reader comics and graphic novels include:

1. An example "Adventure Is Out There!" lesson plan that focuses on readers in kindergarten through second grade (Figure 4.3),

2. An example "Adventure Is Out There!" lesson plan that focuses on readers in third through sixth grade (Figure 4.4),

3. A blank "Adventure Is Out There!" lesson plan for your classroom use (Figure 4.5),

4. A comic book exposé of James Sturm, Andrew Arnold, and Alexis Frederick-Frost's *Adventures in Cartooning: Activity Book* (Figure 4.6), and

5. A comic book exposé of Belle Yang's *Forget Sorrow* (Figure 4.7).

FIGURE 4.3: **"ADVENTURE IS OUT THERE!" FOR READERS IN KINDERGARTEN THROUGH SECOND GRADE (WRITTEN FOR TEACHERS TO EXPLAIN TO THEIR STUDENTS)**

"Adventure is out there!" for Readers in Kindergarten through Second Grade "Adventure is out there!" lets you take your students on a journey of discovery. On this journey, they will learn new things about themselves and the world around them.	
Stage 1: Prepare for your adventure	In order to prepare students for their upcoming adventure, you can begin the lesson by pointing out the various prepared learning stations around the room. Tell students that, in groups of three or four, they will travel to each station. If you have particularly young readers, you may want to give them a preview of what they will find at each station. **Resource material and questions can be found at each station.** **Station 1: Where?** Resources: Large paper, markers, and photocopied pictures of the setting from the early reader comic or graphic novel Question: Where does the story take place? **Station 2: Who?** Resources: Large paper, markers, and photocopied pictures of the characters from the early reader comic or graphic novel Question: Who are the characters in this story? **Station 3: What are some things we might experience on our adventure?** Resources: Large paper, markers, and photocopied pictures of the adventures found in the early reader comic or graphic novel Question: What adventures might we go on in this story? **Station 4: Why is it important for us to go on this adventure?** Resources: Large paper, markers, and photocopied pictures of significant moments from the early reader comic or graphic novel Question: What significant things might we learn on our adventure? When students are done traveling to all of the stations, ask the class to discuss their experiences and/or thoughts about each station.

Stage 2: **Go on your** **adventure**	During stage 2 of "Adventure is out there!" students will keep a travel log. Make numerous copies of Appendix C (blank comic/graphic novel pages) for this travel log, and provide students with pencils and paper. Students' travel logs should record the various adventures they go on while reading the early reader comic or graphic novel. Since these are K-2 readers, I suggest that you keep a travel log as well, modeling the idea for your students. Note: Please remind students that they can keep their travel logs using words, images, or words and images together.
Stage 3: **Share your** **adventure**	When students are finished reading the early reader comic or graphic novel, they need to go back and read their travel log. Explain that, when adventurers return from a journey, they are often asked to share what they have learned. Ask students to choose two of their most significant learning experiences and make a poster—using basic panels, gutters, and balloons—that highlights those two ideas. To wrap up their adventure, ask students to share their posters with the rest of the class.

Note: Teachers will need to provide the resource materials at each station that are needed for this lesson.

	"Adventure is out there!" **"Adventure is out there!" means that you are about to embark on a journey that will call on you to not only discover new ideas about yourself, but also discover new ideas about other people. You are about to go on an exciting adventure of discovery!**
Stage 1: **Prepare for your** **adventure**	In order to prepare for your upcoming adventure, your teacher has prepared learning stations around the room. At each station, your teacher has chosen images and text from the graphic novel that will help you better answer that station's question. In groups of three or four (assigned by your teacher), travel to each station, and answer the questions below. You will have five to ten minutes at each station. **Materials and clues for these questions can be found at each station. Feel free to record your answers in the space below.** **Station 1: Where are we going on our adventure?** **Station 2: Who might we meet on our adventure?** **Station 3: What are some things we might be doing on our adventure?** **Station 4: Why is it important for us to go on this adventure?** When you are finished traveling to all of the stations, discuss your thoughts and experiences from each station.

Stage 2: Go on your adventure	During stage 2 of "Adventure is out there!" you will keep a travel log. You can use blank comic/graphic novel pages (provided by your teacher) for this travel log; teachers, Appendix C provides copy-friendly comic/graphic novel pages for your students to use during this step in their journey. Your travel log will help you record your notes and thoughts about what you are learning and experiencing from the comic or graphic novel you are reading. To write in your travel log you will need paper, a pencil, and markers/crayons. You will write in your travel log three times. Note: You can keep your travel log using words, images, or words and images together. **Before reading** Before you read, leaf through the comic or graphic novel and write about what you might learn about on your upcoming adventure. **During reading** At certain points in your reading, your teacher will ask you to stop reading and write about what you have learned so far. **After reading** When you are finished reading, your teacher will give you time to write and reflect on your entire adventure. Ask yourself what you learned overall on your adventure.
Stage 3: Share your adventure	When you are finished reading the comic or graphic novel, go back and read your entire travel log. When adventurers return from a journey, they are often asked to share what they have learned. Choose two of the most significant learning experiences from your adventure, and—using comic panels, gutters, and balloons—make a poster highlighting those two ideas. Your poster will need to: • Include a title that starts with: *On my adventure, I learned* _____. • Identify two of your most significant learning experiences • Use both words and images to explain what you learned about these two experiences • List the page numbers from the comic or graphic novel that helped you learn about these experiences

Because the multicultural theme "Adventure is out there!" is broad enough to include all types of cultural diversity, I recommend that you not only use Figures 4.3 or 4.4 in your classrooms, but also create your own "Adventure is out there!" lesson ideas. Figure 4.5 offers a blank "Adventure is out there!" handout for just that purpose. I also encourage you to share your ideas on my blog, http://teachinggraphicnovels.blogspot.com.

	"Adventure is out there!"
	"Adventure is out there!" means that you are about to embark on a journey that will call on you to not only discover new ideas about yourself, but also discover new ideas about other people. You are about to go on an exciting adventure of discovery!
Stage 1: Prepare for your adventure	
Stage 2: Go on your adventure	
Stage 3: Share your adventure	

Since this chapter broadly addresses multicultural early reader comics and graphic novels for various elementary grade levels, I will highlight two specific multicultural comics and/or graphic novels—one for kindergarten through third-grade readers and one for fourth- through sixth-grade readers.

Adventures in Cartooning: Activity Book is an excellent multicultural comic for kindergarten through third-grade readers because it helps teachers bridge reading and writing while encouraging multicultural and diverse thinking and learning.

FIGURE 4.6: **MULTICULTURAL EARLY READER COMIC EXPOSÉ OF *ADVENTURES IN CARTOONING: ACTIVITY BOOK* FOR READERS IN KINDERGARTEN THROUGH THIRD GRADE**

Adventures in Cartooning: Activity Book by James Sturm, Andrew Arnold, and Alexis Frederick-Frost (First Second, 2010)

Summary

Adventures in Cartooning: Activity Book encourages early readers to create and write their own comic stories. Students are able to bring their own ideas, thoughts, and beliefs about culture to the table. There are no limits to what the authors of *Adventures in Cartooning: Activity Book* encourage students to explore. Students are culturally empowered to be the authors of whatever cultural adventures they would like to go on!

Interesting information

Comics greatly impacted Alexis Frederick-Frost's childhood, helping him to discover his voice and relate to others:

> "When I was young, I was very socially awkward. I had a hard time finding friends in school and, since I didn't have cable TV or video games at home, I ended up spending a lot of time drawing. I would make up stories to entertain myself or my sister and, at some point, I began showing them to classmates. Surprisingly, these little drawings of knights fighting hordes of monsters or terminators battling on an alien world had some social cache. Comics became a way for me to relate to the kids around me and a way to process events in my life. Their subjects began shifting away from battles to anxieties about tests, experiences I had on class trips, and even stuff I did with friends. Comics were a tool I could use to process, examine, and feel a little more in control of events in my life. I found my own voice through them. In this era where so much of life is seen through media, I think its important to empower young people to tell their own stories, to create their own media, to find their own voices. I believe comics are one of the tools that can be used to do this."

Pages 8 and 9, in particular, provide a schema-building comic background. These two pages provide students with the freedom to explore how their own cultural beliefs, traditions, thoughts, or ideas may influence the story they wish to tell.

FIGURE 4.7: MULTICULTURAL GRAPHIC NOVEL EXPOSÉ OF *FORGET SORROW* FOR READERS IN FOURTH THROUGH SIXTH GRADES

Forget Sorrow by Belle Yang (W. W. Norton & Company, 2010)

Summary

Embarrassed and ashamed to move home after a failed (and dangerous) relationship with a boyfriend that Belle and her parents eventually nickname "Rotten Egg," a young Belle at first has trouble understanding her parents' culturally influenced reactions to this doomed relationship. That is, however, until Belle's father begins to tell her about his own family history growing up in China. Drawing and recording her father's family history leads Belle on a personal and familial journey of discovery, where the meaning behind her Chinese name, *Xuan (forget sorrow)*, breathes new life into the relationship between Belle, her parents, and their ancestral past.

As more and more educators try new ideas and continue to pave the way for teaching multicultural early reader comics and graphic novels, like those mentioned in this chapter, teachers and students will both reap the benefits. I invite you to share success stories at http://teachinggraphicnovels.blogspot.com.

-APPENDIX-

APPENDIX A: BASIC TERMINOLOGY FOR TEACHING EARLY READER COMICS AND GRAPHIC NOVELS

To teach early readers some basic terms for reading comics and graphic novels, teachers will want to highlight the following terms: panel, gutter, and balloon.

Panel: The boundary and the contents within it that tell a piece of the story.

Here's an example of a panel from *Benny and Penny in Just Pretend* (Toon Books, 2008) by Geoffrey Hayes.

In this panel example, Penny is looking for her brother Benny. You can see a visual boundary placed around the piece of the story being told. This boundary constitutes the panel.

Gutter: The space between the panels where readers connect two or more ideas into one idea.

Let's look at some gutter examples from *Luke on the Loose* (Toon Books, 2009) by Harry Bliss.

In the first panel, on the top left, readers see Luke's father reporting his lost son to a policeman. Traveling through the gutter and into the second panel, readers next see Luke's father showing the policeman his son's photo. These two panels are linked from one moment to the next moment, from Luke's father reporting his lost son to Luke's father showing the policeman a photo of his son.

Balloons: Usually found inside of a panel, balloons typically create visual boundaries that progress the story in terms of dialogue, thought, and/or sound.

Here's an example of a grouping of balloons from *Adventures in Cartooning* (First Second, 2009) by James Sturm, Andrew Arnold, and Alexis Frederick-Frost.

In this example, the knight has specific ideas, each of which manifests itself in a balloon. The magic elf is also shown with some balloons.

APPENDIX B: ADVANCED, LAYERED TERMINOLOGY FOR TEACHING EARLY READER COMICS AND GRAPHIC NOVELS

Panel: The visual or implied boundary and the contents within it that tell a piece of the story.

Using the *Benny and Penny* panel example from the previous section, let's take a more in-depth look at how panels relate to what we have traditionally taught in ELA.

When we bring our understanding of teaching ELA together with a new understanding of and appreciation for early reader comic and graphic novel panels, we can link the teaching of panels with the teaching of the elements of a story.

For advanced early readers, there are seven types of story panels.

SEVEN TYPES OF STORY PANELS FOUND IN EARLY READER COMICS AND GRAPHIC NOVELS

Examples taken from *Benny and Penny in Just Pretend* (Toon Books, 2008) by Geoffrey Hayes.

1. **Plot panels: These panels develop the main set of events that unfold in early reader comics or graphic novels.**

On this first page, Penny is shown looking for her brother, Benny. This initial search is the first in a sequence of events that progresses the storyline.

2. Character panels: These panels focus on and develop individual or multiple characters.

While Benny wants Penny to take her nap and leave him alone, Penny would like to stay and play. A healthy dose of sibling rivalry is clearly at play between these two characters.

3. Setting panels: These panels develop setting, the place(s) where the graphic novel takes place.

While Benny is hidden in his pirate cave, Penny is looking for him from above, near the large tree. The reader can also see that, due to a spider, Benny is about to move to another, new setting in upcoming panels.

4. Conflict panels: These panels develop the source of conflict in the graphic novel, the tension that motivates the story.

In this conflict-focused panel, Benny is revealing the primary tension that runs throughout this story—that he would like to play pirate alone, without his sister.

5. Rising action panels: These panels develop the set of events that stem from the conflict, give rise to that conflict, and lead to the climax in the graphic novel.

Developing the action in the story, Benny tells Penny that he wants to play hide-and-seek. However, in reality, Benny just wants to get away from Penny so he again can play pirate by himself.

6. Climax panels: These panels develop the point of greatest intensity in the story.

After feeling poorly about leaving Penny in the box, Benny goes in search of his sister, and they agree to play "hide-and-seek" together. In these climactic panels, Penny actually proves herself to be much braver than Benny had assumed.

7. Resolution panels: These panels develop the final outcome that solves the primary conflict(s) in the graphic novel.

In the resolution panels, Benny apologizes to Penny.

Gutter: The space between the panels; here, in the limbo of the gutter, human imagination takes over and discovers a logical bridge from one panel to the next panel.

For readers in kindergarten through third grade, I recommend that you refer to the term "gutter" alone.

For readers in grades four through six, however, I recommend that you not only refer to the term "gutter," but also to the five most common types of gutters.

FIVE COMMON TYPES OF GUTTERS

Moment-to-moment gutter: From one panel to the next, readers witness little closure and instead simply see something from one instance to another.

In this example, the reader sees Luke's dad from one moment to the next, first with his cell phone ringing, then as he answers the phone, and, finally, as he begins to talk on the phone.

Examples taken from *Luke on the Loose* (Toon Books, 2009) by Harry Bliss.

Action-to-action gutter: Between these panels, readers see a single subject going through specific transitions.

These gutter sequences show the action generated from Luke chasing the dog.

Subject-to-subject gutter: While sticking with a single idea, these panels move the reader from one subject to the next, often progressing the storyline. McCloud reminds us to "note the degree of reader involvement necessary to render these transitions meaningful" (71).

In the first panel, Luke is the subject. In the second panel, however, Luke's father is the subject.

Scene-to-scene gutter: In reading these panels, readers often need to exercise deductive reasoning, for these panels move the reader across "significant distances of time and space" (McCloud, p. 71, 1993).

The reader moves from the first panel, focusing on Luke's mom as the subject, to the second panel, focusing on Luke as the subject.

Aspect-to-aspect gutter: Because these gutters ask readers to think about the feelings or emotions being conveyed from one panel to the next, they are comparable to tone or mood.

In the top three panels that overlay the larger panel page, the reader gets a sense of the flat or boring parent-to-parent conversational tone. In the page-sized panel, however, the reader gets quite a different tone or mood from Luke—one of excitement.

Note: Students should be encouraged to notice that some gutters can have multiple labels.

Balloons: Usually found inside of a panel, balloons are typically used to create visual boundaries that progress the story in terms of dialogue, thought, and/or sound.

Just like with gutters, for readers in kindergarten through third grade, I recommend that you refer to the term "balloon" alone.

For readers in grades four through six, however, I recommend that you not only refer to the term "balloon," but also to the five most common types of balloons.

FIVE COMMON TYPES OF EARLY READER COMIC AND GRAPHIC NOVEL BALLOONS

Story balloons: Balloons that focus on progressing the storyline/plot.

In these balloons, the reader learns that Otto's favorite color is orange and that, according to Otto, the world would be boring without it.

Example taken from *Otto's Orange Day* (Toon Books, 2009) by Frank Cammuso and Jay Lynch.

Thought balloons: Balloons that focus on a character's thoughts/ideas.

In this thought balloon, which contains a light bulb image, the reader can see that the young knight has thought of an idea.

Example taken from *Adventures in Cartooning* (First Second, 2009) by James Sturm, Andrew Arnold, and Alexis Frederick-Frost.

Dialogue balloons: Balloons that focus on conversation between characters or one character speaking aloud to him/herself.

In these dialogue balloon examples, the reader can see Kaput and Zösky talking about the planet Earth and their desire to get rid of it and eat all the chocolate desserts.

Example taken from *Kaput and Zösky* (First Second, 2008) by Lewis Trondheim and Eric Cartier.

Sound effect balloons: Balloons that use words or images to convey a sense of sound.

Example taken from *Mo and Jo: Fighting Together Forever* (Toon Books, 2008) by Dean Haspiel and Jay Lynch.

Each of these two panels contains a sound effect balloon, with a third sound effect balloon sitting right in between them. They allow the reader to not only hear the characters' grunts as they pull on a costume, but also the rip of the costume as it tears into two pieces.

Balloon-less balloons: Spaces within a panel that have implied boundaries; the balloon-less balloon may also serve any of the aforementioned functions (e.g., a balloon-less story balloon, a balloon-less thought balloon, a balloon-less dialogue balloon).

This balloon-less balloon simply exists within the panel and, due to its focus on purely progressing the storyline, is a story balloon.

Example taken from *Adventures in Cartooning* (First Second, 2009) by James Sturm, Andrew Arnold, and Alexis Frederick-Frost.

Note: Students should be encouraged to notice that some balloons can have multiple labels.

APPENDIX D: **WHAT COMIC COMES NEXT?**

Directions: After reading and discussing all of the significant events from the comic or graphic novel, work in small groups to decide upon the three MOST important events. Document your choices in the three panels below using words, images, or words and images together. In the gutters between each panel, explain why you chose the previous panel. You can also feel free to add balloons to each panel.

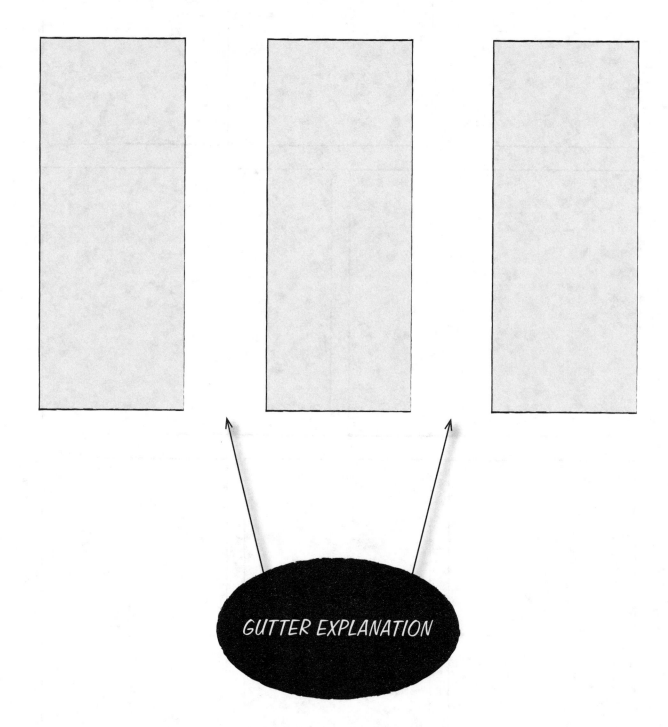

GUTTER EXPLANATION

-BIBLIOGRAPHY-

Abadzis, N. (2007). *Laika*. New York: First Second Books.

Abel, J., & Madden, M. (2008). *Drawing words and writing pictures*. New York: First Second Books.

Adventures of Digger and friends, the. (2010). San Diego, CA: IDW.

Anderson, Ho Che. (2010). *King: The special edition*. Seattle, WA: Fantagraphics.

Azzarello, Brian, Bermejo, L. (2005). *Lex Luthor: Man of steel*. New York: DC Comics.

Bailey, N. (2009). *Female Force*. Beverly Hills, CA: Bluewater Productions.

Baumann, M., & Katschke, J. (2006). *Phonics comics: Duke and Fang – level 3*. Norwalk, CT: Innovative Kids.

Bliss, H. (2009). *Luke on the loose*. New York: Toon Books.

Bitz, M. (2009). *Manga high: Literacy, identity, and coming of age in an urban high school*. Cambridge, MA: Harvard Education Press.

Bitz, M. (2010). *When commas meet kryptonite: Classrooms lessons from the Comic Book Project*. New York: TCP.

Buckingham, D. (2003). *Media education: Literacy, learning and contemporary culture*. Malden, MA: Polity.

Busiek, K., & Immonen, S. (2005). *Superman: Secret identity*. London, UK: Titan Books.

Butzer, C.M. (2009). *Gettysburg: The graphic novel*. New York: HarperCollins.

Cammuso, F. (2008). *Knights of the lunch table*. New York: Scholastic.

Cammuso, F. (2010). *Otto's orange day*. New York: Toon Books.

Carter, J.B. (2007). *Building literacy connections with graphic novels*. Urbana, IL: NCTE.

Carter, J.B., Evensen, E. (2011). *Super-powered word study*. Gainesville, FL: Maupin House.

Colbert, C.C., & Tanitoc. (2010). *Booth*. New York: First Second.

Colfer, E., Donkin, A., & Rigano, G. (2007). *Artemis Fowl: The graphic novel*. New York, NY: Hyperion.

Collins, P., & Burns, C. (2010). *The quest of Perseus*. Coppell, TX: Educators Publishing Service.

Craft, J. (2007). *Mama's boyz: Home schoolin'*. New York: Mama's Boyz, Inc.

Davis, E. (2008). *Stinky*. New York: Toon Books.

Dembicki, M. (2010). *Trickster*. Golden, CO: Fulcrum.

Eisner, W. (1978). *A Contract with God*. New York: Norton.

Eisner, W. (1985). *Comics and sequential art*. Tamarac, FL: Poorhouse.

Eisner, W. (1996). *Graphic storytelling and visual narrative*. Tamarac, FL: Poorhouse.

Fountas, I.C., & Pinnell, G.S. (2001). *Guiding readers and writers*. Portsmouth, NH: Heinemann.

Gaiman, N. (1993). *The books of magic*. New York: DC Comics.

Gallagher, J. (2006). *Buzzboy: Sidekicks rule!*. Falls Church, VA: Sky-Dog Comics.

Gardner, H. (1983). *Frames of mind: The theory of multiple intelligences*. New York: Basic Books.

Gee, J.P. (2003). *What videogames have to teach us about learning and literacy*. New York: Palgrave.

Gownley, J. (2006). *Amelia rules! Superheroes*. Harrisburg, PA: Renaissance Press.

Gravel, E. (2010). *Balloon toons: Adopt a glurb*. Maplewood, NJ: Blue Apple Books.

Guibert, E., & Sfar, J. (2006). *Sardine in outer space*. New York: First Second.

Guthrie, J.T. & Wigfield, A. (2000). Engagement and motivation in reading. In M.L. Kamil, P.B. Mosenthal, P.D. Pearson, & R. Barr (Eds.), *Handbook of reading research: Volume III* (pp. 403-422). New York: Erlbaum.

Hajdu, D. (2008). *The ten-cent plague: The great comic-book scare and how it changed America*. New York: FSG.

Haspiel, D., & Lynch, J. (2008). *Mo and Jo: Fighting together forever*. New York: Toon Books.

Hatke, B. (2010). *Zita the spacegirl*. New York: First Second.

Hayes, G. (2010). *Benny and Penny in just pretend*. New York: First Second.

Hobbs, R. (2007). *Reading the media: Media literacy in high school English*. New York: Teachers College Press.

Holm, J., & Castaldi, E. (2007). *Middle school is worse than meatloaf*. New York: Simon & Schuster.

Holm, J., & Holm, M. (2005). *Babymouse*. New York: Random House.

Hull, G., & Schultz, K. (2002). *School's out: Bridging out-of-school literacies with classroom practice*. New York: Teachers College Press.

Jablonski, C., & Purvis, L. (2010). *Resistance book 1*. New York: First Second.

Johnson, S. (2005). *Everything bad is good for you*. New York: Riverhead.

Kelly, J. (2010). *Four eyes volume 1: Forged in flames*. Berkeley, CA: IMAGE.

Kibuishi, K. (2008). *Amulet: Book one: The stonekeeper*. New York: Scholastic.

Kinney, J. (2007). *Diary of a wimpy kid*. New York: Abrams.

Kist, W. (2004). *New literacies in action*. New York: TCP.

Kist, W. (2010). *The socially networked classroom: Teaching in the new media age*. Thousand Oaks, CA: Corwin.

Klein, G. (2006). *The lost colony, book one: The Snodgrass conspiracy*. New York: First Second.

Kress, G. (2003). *Literacy in the new media age*. New York: Routledge.

Krosoczka, J. (2009). *Lunch lady and the league of librarians*. New York: Random House.

Laird, R., Laird, T.N., & Bey, Elihu "Adofo." (2009). *Still I rise: A graphic history of African Americans*. New York: Sterling.

Langer, J. (1989). Thinking and doing literature: An eight-year study. *English Journal*, 87(2). 16-23. Urbana, IL: NCTE.

Larson, H. (2008). *Chiggers*. New York: Simon & Schuster.

Lockjaw and the pet avengers. (2010). New York: Marvel.

Long, E. (2010). *Balloon toons: Rick & Rack and the great outdoors*. Maplewood, NJ: Blue Apple Books.

Lyga, B. (2009). *Wolverine: Worst day ever*. New York: Marvel.

Masterman, L. (1985). *Teaching the media*. New York: Routledge.

McCann, J., Lee, J. (2010). *The return of the dapper men*. Hollywood, CA: Archaia.

McCloud, S. (2006). *Making comics: Storytelling secrets of comics, manga and graphic novels*. New York: HarperCollins.

McCloud, S. (2000). *Reinventing comics: How imagination and technology are revolutionizing an art form*. New York: HarperCollins.

McCloud, S. (1993). *Understanding comics: The invisible art*. New York: HarperCollins.

McCulloch, D., & Robinson, J. (2009). *T. runt*. Berkeley, CA: IMAGE.

McDonald, M., & Reynolds, P. (2005). *Stink: The incredible shrinking kid*. Somerville, MA: Candlewick.

McKenna, M., & Kear, D. (1990). Measuring attitude toward reading: A new tool for teachers. *The Reading Teacher*, 46, 626 – 639.

McLeod, B. (2008). *SuperHero ABC*. New York: HarperCollins.

McLuhan, M. (1964). *Understanding media: The extensions of man*. New York: McGraw-Hill.

Mechner, J., Sina, A.B., Pham, L., & Puvilland, A. (2008). *Prince of Persia: The graphic novel*. New York: First Second.

Medley, L. (2006). *Castle waiting*. Seattle, WA: Fantagraphics.

Mignola, M. (1994). *Hellboy*. Milwaukie, OR: Dark Horse.

Millar, M., Johnson, D., Plunkett, K., Robinson, A., & Wong, W. (2003). *Superman: Red son*. New York: DC.

Monnin, K. (2010). *Teaching graphic novels*. Gainesville, FL: Maupin House.

Moore, C. McAdams, & Dammer, M. (2007). *Phonics comics: Cave Dave – Level 1*. Norwalk, CT: Innovative Kids.

Moss, M. (2009). *Max disaster #1: Alien eraser to the rescue*. Somerville, MA: Candlewick.

Newsom Report, The. (1963). *Half our future*. London: HMSO.

New London Group, The. (1996). A pedagogy of multi-literacies: Designing social futures. *Harvard Educational Review*, 66.1, 60-92.

Niles, S., & Roman, B. (2008). *The cryptics*. San Diego, CA: IDW.

O'Connor, G., & Van den Bogaert, H.M. (2006). *Journey into Mohawk country*. New York, NY: First Second.

Parker, J. (2010). *Missile mouse: The star crusher*. New York: Scholastic.

Patterson, J., & Gout, L. (2008). *Daniel X: Alien hunter*. St. Louis, MO: Turtleback.

Petersen, D. (2009). *Mouse guard volume 1: Fall 1152*. Hollywood, CA: Archaia.

Petrucha, S., & Murase, S. (2005). *Nancy Drew, girl detective #1: The demon of River Heights*. New York: Papercutz.

Peyo. (2010). *The smurf king*. New York: Papercutz.

Renier, A. (2010). *The unsinkable Walker Bean*. New York: First Second.

Renier, A. (2005). *Spiral-bound*. Marietta, GA: Top Shelf.

Roman, D. (2011). *Astronaut academy: Zero gravity*. New York: First Second.

Rosenstiehl, A. (2010). *Silly Lilly and the four seasons*. New York: Toon Books.

Sava, S.C., & Jourdan, D. (2008). *Ed's terrestrials*. San Diego, CA: IDW.

Sava, S.C., & Mourges, J.S. (2009). *My grandparents are secret agents*. San Diego, CA: IDW.

Schwarz, G. (2002). Graphic novels for multiple literacies. *Journal of Adolescent & Adult Literacy*, 46.3, 262-65. Newark, DE: IRA.

Schweizer, C. (2008). *Crogan's vengeance (Crogan adventures 1)*. Portland, OR: Oni.

Selznick, B. (2007). *The invention of Hugo Cabaret*. New York: Scholastic.

Sendak, M. (1963). *Where the wild things are*. New York: HarperCollins.

Sendak, M. (1971). *In the night kitchen*. New York: HarperCollins.

Shiga, J. (2010). *Meanwhile: Pick any path, 3, 856 story possibilities*. New York: Amulet.

Simon, K.K., Valentino, J., & Butterworth, A. (2008). *Bruce: The little blue spruce*. Berkeley, CA: IMAGE.

Smith, J. (2005). *Bone*. New York: Scholastic.

Smith, J., & Sniegoski, T. (2010). *Bone: Tall tales*. New York: Scholastic.

Smith, J., & Sniegoski, T. (2011). *Bone: Quest for the spark: Book one*. New York: GRAPHIX.

Soo, K. (2008). *Jellaby*. New York: Hyperion.

Soo, K. (2009). *Jellaby: Monster in the city*. New York: Hyperion.

Spiegelman, A. (2008). *Jack in the box*. New York: Toon Books.

Spiegelman, A. (1986). *Maus I*. New York: Pantheon.

Spiegelman, A. (1991). *Maus II*. New York: Pantheon.

Spiegelman, A., Mouly, F., Eds. (2006). *Big fat little lit*. New York: Puffin.

Spiegelman, A., & Mouly, F., Eds. (2009). *The toon treasury of classic children's comics*. New York: Abrams.

Stamaty, Mark Alan. (2004). *Alia's Mission*. New York: Knopf.

Star wars: Clone wars adventures: Volume 1. (2004). Milwaukie, OR: Dark Horse.

Stassen, J.P., & Siegel, A. (2006). *Deogratias: A tale of Rwanda*. New York: First Second.

Steinke, A. N. (2010). *Balloon toons: The super crazy cat dance*. Maplewood, NJ: Blue Apple.

Sturm, J., Tommaso, R. (2007). *Satchel Paige: Striking out Jim Crow*. New York: Hyperion.

Sturm, J., Arnold, A., & Frederick-Frost, A. (2009). *Adventures in cartooning*. New York: First Second.

Sturm, J., Arnold, A., & Frederick-Frost, A. (2010). *Adventures in cartooning: Activity book*. New York: First Second.

Telgemeier, R. (2006). *The babysitter's club: Kristy's great idea*. New York: Scholastic.

Telgemeier, R. (2010). *Smile*. New York: Scholastic.

TenNapel, D. (2005). *Tommysaurus rex*. Berkeley, CA. IMAGE.

TenNapel, D. (2007). *Earthboy Jacobus*. Berkeley, CA: IMAGE.

TenNapel, D. (2007). *Flink*. Berkeley, CA: IMAGE.

TenNapel, D. (2010). *Ghostopolis*. New York: Scholastic.

Tezuka, O. (2006). *Buddha: Volume 1*. New York: Vertical.

Trine, G., & Montijo, R. (2006). *The curse of the bologna sandwich (Melvin Beederman, superhero)*. New York: Henry Holt.

Trondheim, L., & Cartier, E. (2008). *Kaput and Zösky*. New York: First Second.

Trondheim, L., & Parme, F. (2009). *Tiny tyrant: Volume one*. New York: First Second.

Varon, S. (2006). *Chicken and cat*. New York: Scholastic.

Veron, U. (2009). *Dragonbreath*. New York: Penguin.

Waid, M., Yu, Leinil F., & Alanguilan, G. *Superman: Birthright*. New York: DC.

Wax, W., & Sullivan, M. (2007). *Phonics comics: Clara the klutz – level 2*. Norwalk, CT: Innovative Kids.

Werthman, F. (1954). *Seduction of the innocent*. New York: Rinehart.

Wight, E. (2010). *Frankie Pickle and the pine run 3000*. New York: Simon & Schuster.

Williamson, J., & Navarrete, V. (2008). *Dear Dracula*. Berkeley, CA: IMAGE.

Yang, B. (2010). *Forget sorrow*. New York: Norton.

Yang, G. L. (2006). *American born Chinese*. New York: First Second.

Yang, G. L. (2009). *Prime baby*. New York: First Second.

Yolen, J. & Cavallaro, M. (2010). *Foiled*. New York: First Second.

Zimmerman, B. (2010). *Your life in comics*. Minneapolis, MN: Free Spirit Press.

-INDEX-